White Water Landings

A view of the Imperial Airways Africa service from the ground

J M PETT
memoir by
GEOFFREY PETT

Foreword by Gordon Pirie

White Water Landings
J M Pett with Geoffrey Pett
Published by Princelings Publications, Norwich, Norfolk
Blurb edition (paperback) v1.0

Copyright © 2016 J M Pett
All rights reserved.

DEDICATION

For my brothers,
and all my parents' grandchildren
and great-grandchildren

CONTENTS

Acknowledgments
Foreword
Introduction – M'beriali 1

Part 1   **The Golden Age of Flying**

1. Early Days and Recruitment 7
2. Commercial Trainee 12
3. Brindisi 22
4. Centaurus 29
5. Nairobi 36
6. Station Superintendent 42
7. Lindi 54
8. Butiaba 90
9. Have station, will travel 95
10. Juba and the Rejaf station 102
11. The Corsair Affair 119
12. Life at Juba 126
13. Early 1939 138
14. The summer of 1939 144

Part 2   **Love and War**

15. Imperial Airways HQ on evacuation 151
16. Alexandria and Cairo 154
17. Return to Juba 163
18. Khartoum and Wadi Saidna 176
19. Cairo and Kampala 188
20. The End of the Story 204

Postscript 208
Appendix: Postings 209
Bibliography 211
Index 213

List of Illustrations

	Imperial Airways Africa Route 1940
	(Illustration by Danielle English)
1	*Calpurnia* AETW at Lindi
8	Faversham Grammar School football team 1931-32
	(Geoffrey seated on leftmost chair)
13	Geoffrey Pett, c1934
17	Croydon Airport c1934
24	Brindisi – Albergo Internationale
28	*Satyrus* at Brindisi
30	Holiday at Whitstable, Kent 1936
35	*Centaurus* at Alexandria (courtesy of Mark Postlethwaite)
37	HP42, Hannibal or Heracles class, G-AAXC
39	Giraffe in the bush
40	Rhinoceros
43	Elephant herd in the Serengeti
45	Mbeya, dawn take-off
47	Mbeya station resthouse 1937
51	Mbeya, Atalanta in the noon-day sun
53	Mbeya, Atalanta G-ABTL
55	Lindi beach
58	Geoffrey Pett, Lindi 1937
61	Lindi station
63	IAL launch under cover, Lindi
65	*Centurion* ADVE lands at Lindi
66	AEU? Coming in at Lindi
68	Lindi native staff
70	Social life at Lindi
73	Lindi IAL office
74	*Camilla* AEUB flying out of Lindi
76	Radio Operator, Mark Ray or Mike Murphy
78	*Circe* AETZ lands at Lindi 1937
79	Locals at work

81	The Shell barge, Lindi
83	African native village, near Lindi
87	*Coriolanus* AETV at Lindi
88	*Calpurnia* AETW at Lindi
91	Butiaba, Lake Albert
93	*Canopus* ADHL landing on Lake Albert, March 1938
94	W/O 'Paddy' Coussans, *Canopus* at Butiaba
96	The long tow behind SS *Corynton*
97	Launch and barge lashed alongside SS *Lugard*
98	Nimule: Government resthouse
101	Launches loaded for road transport
103	Geoffrey bush-whacking at Rejaf
105	Prison labour bush-whacking
106	Hippo run to the river Nile
107	Crossing the swamp to Rejaf station
109	Resting during the survey work at Rejaf
110	Boys building the Rejaf 'terminal'
111	The finished terminal!
112	*Corinna* AEUC arrives at Rejaf (Juba)
113	*Corinna* moored at Rejaf
114	Elephant spoor
117	Rejaf (Juba) station c October 1938
121	*Corsair* ADVB crashed on River Dangu, Faradge
123	*Corsair* beached and unloaded
127	Geoffrey Pett, Juba autumn 1938
130	Juba Hotel, Juba
131	View of the pool at Juba Hotel
132	Geoffrey at work in the IAL office, Juba Hotel
135	Geoffrey posing by the pool
139	*Cambria* ADUV at Rejaf (Juba)
140	The 'new' terminal, Juba (Rejaf)
145	Geoffrey with 'Miranda' at Tankerton, Kent, summer 1939
146	Camping with Pat, Marjorie, Mollie, Mabel with David Earl, and John Hutchinson

153	Frances (Mollie) Hutchinson, nurse at the Middlesex Hospital, London
161	Geoffrey with Turkish delegates at Heliopolis, Cairo. 1941. Robert Maxwell may be the one with the hat
167	Juba Hotel: IAL Office (L) and 'tuckle' mess (R, with station wagon)
171	Party with station wagon, possibly for trip to Mongalla
173	Mongalla
177	Geoffrey's RAF pass for Wadi Saidna
178	Geoffrey at Wadi Saidna bungalow
189	Geoffrey at Cairo apartment
196	Wedding party, 2nd April 1943: Mrs McHugh probably in spotted dress next to Geoffrey, Flight Lt. Morris Walter on right of Frances, with probably David Paton in front, holding bush helmet.
198	Frances at Jinja on honeymoon
206	Aileen and Jimmy Druce, friend, and Frances at Gezira Club, Cairo, 1944

All photographs (except where stated) are from the collection of Geoffrey Pett. Copyright is held by his executors.

For permission to use any of these photographs, see the website whitewaterlandings.co.uk

ACKNOWLEDGMENTS

This memoir was inspired by a number of Imperial Airways and flying boat enthusiasts, all desiring to interview the stalwarts of that period about events long past. Their interest in my father's experiences caused him to set his own story down on tape, dictating it over a period of ten years.

My particular thanks go to John Buchan, who was corresponding with Geoffrey at the time of his death and enabled me to get started. John in turn led me to friends of my parents I would have otherwise missed; Aileen Druce, whom I met when I was a child, filled in some of the mysterious gaps towards the end of the story for which we children had only patchy answers.

I would also like to thank my brother James for his untiring help and support, and all those who commented on the website version when I was first transcribing the tapes. Among many I must single out for thanks are Gordon Pirie, whose academic viewpoint has enriched a Foreword that sets the story in its correct historical and cultural context, and the conservation or archival interest of the Croydon Airport Society. Your enthusiasm prompted this book.
I hope you enjoy it.

FOREWORD
by Professor Gordon Pirie, University of Cape Town

Geoffrey Pett's recollections of his work as an *Imperial Airways* ground services employee in the 1930s in Africa are a remarkable and significant piece of aviation and colonial history. His daughter Jacky's painstaking transcriptions from Geoffrey's intermittent tape recordings in his eighties bring to life little-known facets of overseas life and service for Britain's flagship airline between the two world wars. At the time commercial passenger services across Africa were in their infancy. On a wider canvas, his words and the accompanying photographs enrich late colonial historiography. One photo of Geoffrey is also an incidental and compelling image of colonial masculinity and colonial rule: a hatted and robed male servant with silver tray, glass of water and calling card or message tries to attract attention at the margins of a group of men locked tightly by conversation, suits, status and smoke.

After a period as an *Imperial Airways* trainee in London, Croydon, Southampton and Brindisi, Geoffrey's various postings in Egypt, the Sudan, Kenya, Uganda and Tanganyika were to establish, organise and manage the airline's refuelling, navigation, refreshment and overnight accommodation services on its trans-African route. The responsibilities he had in his twenties for safe and smooth airline operations were extraordinary; the technical, logistical, managerial and social ingenuity expected of uniformed young men in the bush and in colonial capital cities and towns was astonishing. Shining through his memoirs is a capacity to 'make do' with erratic and primitive provisioning and communications (including radio, maps and charts), an ingrained sense of responsibility to the airline company, and the sense of the *Imperial* 'family' as a source of identity, support and obligation away from home. Fulfilment at work dominates Geoffrey's story, but his is not a saccharine 'whitewash' of imperial servitude: he reveals anxiety and frustration, exhibits some cynicism for arbitrary authority, and learned to make privilege and isolation work.

Geoffrey's words are a superb record of the rhythms and registers of the 1930s, their transplantation into Africa, and their durability or adaptability after landing there. His consciousness of social class and race is evident; the coyness and awkwardness of gender and love is of the period; the heat of the day is palpable; the sensibility of the hotel and club used by expatriates is transparent; the adventure of motoring and feel of wilderness is striking. Unique 'insider' photographs capture the atmosphere, society, constructions, and work tasks at *Imperial's* stations which Geoffrey helped build from scratch. His daughter's book is a fine tribute.

The Petts' view from the ground is a rare and invaluable treasure about people and (new) technology, their robustness and their mutual dependence. Told fondly, plainly and modestly, with touches of humour, Geoffrey's story reads easily and lingers long. The text is equally delightful as family history, autobiography, and colonial history. There is war-time history too, in which civil aviation activities in   Africa are subsumed into milita operations, and old airline favours and friendships are called on.

As a contribution to knowledge about fledgling civil air transport, *White Water Landings* is a peerless revelation of its experimental and tentative organisation on the ground at imperial outstations over six or so years. A modest tape recording device, and Jacky's diligence, have generated important insights into how an airline which Africans called *M'beriali* hinged on operations steered by Geoffrey and his kind at intermediate landing places like Butiaba, Juba, Lindi, and Rejaf, as well as in London, Cairo and Nairobi. Transposing British Airways' present pilot-dominated motto, Geoffrey and other ground staff may have preferred 'To Serve. To Fly'.

Gordon Pirie
Cape Town
November 2013

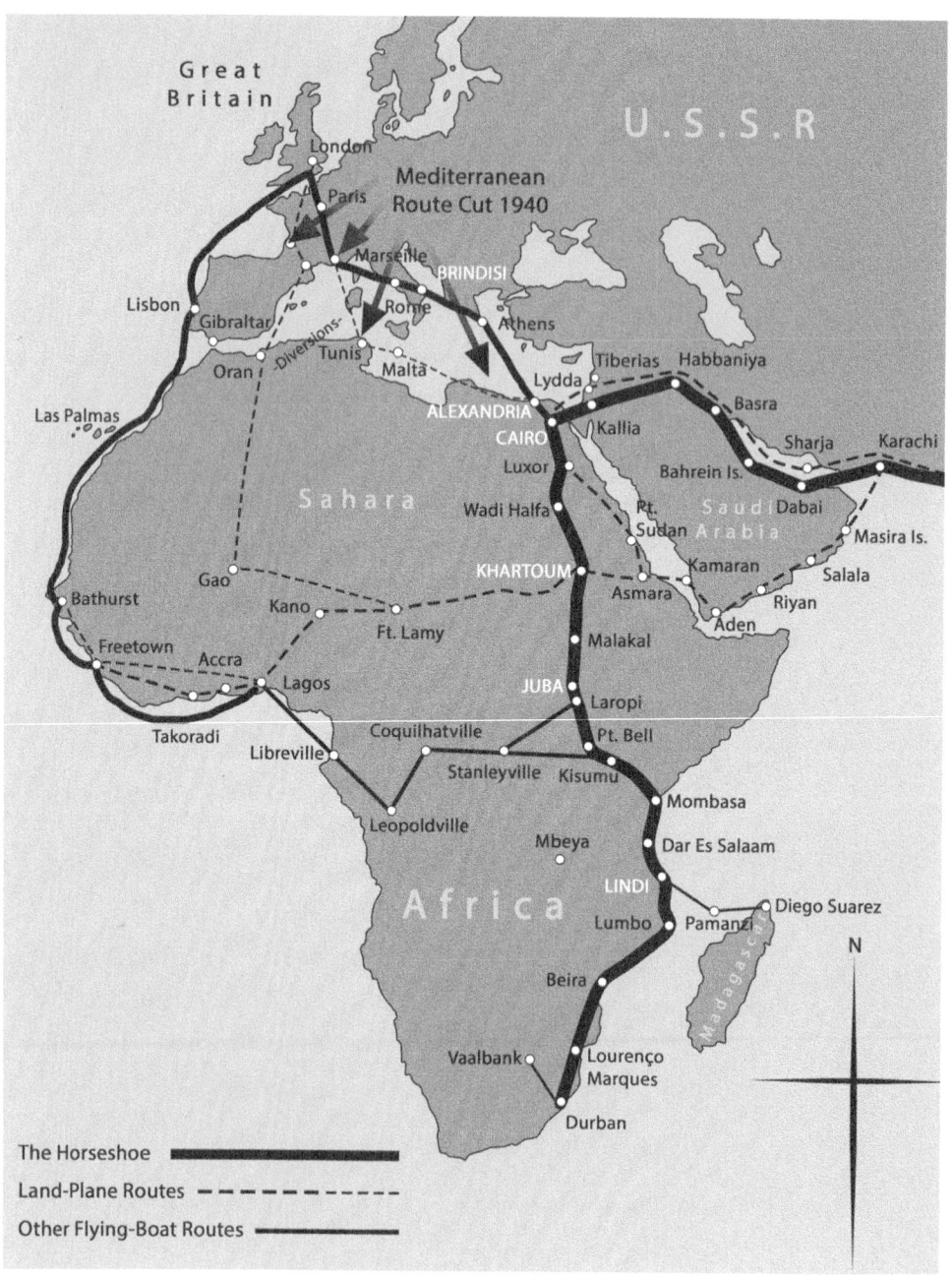

Imperial Airways Africa Route 1940

Introduction – *M'beriali*

The noise of the engines whispered over the African landscape, growing louder as it headed towards the anxious listeners on the coast. They had laboured weeks for this, but only weeks, when some said it would take months. The mooring was marked out with buoys, bobbing in the gentle tide of the Indian Ocean. The coxswain was in the tender, dressed smartly in Imperial Airways tropical kit, ready to guide their visitor to safety. The station superintendent shaded his eyes and searched the skies.

A dark shape materialised and grew into a plane, on course, ready to sweep over their heads and turn over the sea. The throbbing of the engines and the turbulence from the wings seemed to buffet the onlookers, although it was far enough above them to have little real effect.

The silver bird straightened up and sank lower, lower, until it met the sea with a sleek spray that rushed past the windows in its fuselage, so that the passengers could see nothing of the little town of Lindi until they were nearly at the jetty. The local workers stood smartly at the side, waiting until the formalities were over to show their jubilation at the new bird that had visited them.

M'beriali – the imperial mail bird as it was dubbed in Swahili – had arrived. This was its first full journey from Alexandria to the Cape, the southern route of the Imperial Airways Flying Boat service.

For twenty-two year old Geoffrey Pett, just six months into his adventure in the African continent for Imperial Airways, the arrival was both beautiful and a relief. He had done it! Further postings would see him setting up the Imperial Airways landings at Rejaf, near Juba in South Sudan, as well as moving troops around the continent while stationed in Cairo, Egypt in the 1940s. But this day, in the lovely town of Lindi, Tangyanika, with its coconut palms swaying in the wind and the neat lawns marked by white-painted stones round the bungalows of the Government staff stationed there, was a day he'd remember all his life.

More than fifty years were to pass before he started to put his recollections on tape. He was prompted by one of the many journalists and authors who contacted him during his retirement to ask about his memories of the Flying Boat service and Imperial Airways in Africa. His stories were well-honed by telling them through the years to interested colleagues and aviation fans, as well as his family. Meal-times were peppered with stories while the children were growing up, and as time drew closer to running out, they returned with new insights as his now middle-aged children listened just as avidly. So this is how this biography, archive, adventure story, call it what you will, came into being. A set of tapes dictated over ten or more years, a daughter with a penchant for writing and an imagination captured by the mystique of flying boats, and the opportunity provided by modern publishing methods. It combines story telling by Geoffrey with the sort of cutting and editing that he didn't have the patience or the will to do, bound by a narrative drawn by his daughter. There may be mistakes of transcription of proper names, and of Swahili terms, but these have been checked where possible. Are there mistakes of memory? Probably. Geoffrey realised he was telling anecdotes out of sequence on his later tapes. But does that really matter? It is still a valuable record of what life was like for a young man in the 1930s, living in England and colonial Africa, watching the flying boats land, processing the passengers, and ensuring that Imperial Airways 'did its stuff'!

The story takes us from a childhood in the First World War through recruiting the class of 1933 for Imperial Airways' Commercial Trainees. It uncovers the truth about information gathered on enemy boat movement in and out of Brindisi, Italy, and supplies remarkable detail of the commissioning of *Centaurus*, Short C Class flying boat G-ADUT. It tells how to get to the middle of Africa when you cannot fly at night and can only just get high enough to clear the mountains. And once in Africa, it takes you from one romance to another: the dream of first-class commercial aviation to the reality of hitching a lift in the bomb-sighting position of a friendly SAAF plane after you've finally managed to meet up with your bride and get married.

Geoffrey's narrative reflects the language and culture of his time. Sometimes there are phrases that do not sit well with current sensibilities, in particular references to the native staff as 'boys'. He did find it incongruous, to be speaking of people much older than him in such a way, but such was the style of his time. No disrespect is intended to any people, groups or ethnicities.

The tale stops before the end. Geoffrey hadn't finished the story of Cairo in the war and how he came home, before he succumbed to illness in 2005. Some of that has been added by friends and family. But most of the flying is done, the adventures are over, and the romance of Imperial Airways already confined to the past, since during the Second World War it had already been merged into what was to become, many years later, British Airways.

So, how did it all start, in Geoffrey's words?

PART ONE:

The Golden Age of Flying

Chapter 1:
Early days and Recruitment

Geoffrey was born on 24th June 1915 in Throwley in Kent, where his father was the village bobby (policeman). His father was transferred to Faversham (a market town about three and a half miles away from Throwley) a year or so later, where they lived in a house in Preston Avenue. His brother Denis was two years older than him, and his sister, Maureen, six years younger.

The earliest thing I remember was a searchlight. It was the searchlight showing up the zeppelin which raided the Thames estuary in about 1916, but I was very small, I was in my mother's arms and I was wrapped up in a blanket, and she was holding me out in the front of the house that we lived in. I remember that very clearly.

Another memory of Preston Avenue: one day when the milkman was delivering milk. In those days the milkman's float was horse-drawn; he used to come along with great churns of milk and mother used to put a jug out for a pint or quart of milk. The milkman would take the jug, open the valve on the churn, and measure out the milk that mother wanted and leave it on the doorstep or knock. But on this day, as he was bringing the milk to the house, the maroon went off!

The maroon was a great signal that shot up into the air and exploded with an enormous bang! And that indicated that there was a fire. The fire engine was horse-drawn too. When the maroon went off, everyone that volunteered for the fire fighting service dashed down to the fire station, collecting the horses as they went. They buckled them on to the fire engine and off they went to wherever the fire was.

On this particular occasion, the maroon went off when the milkman was in our house. The horse heard the bang and dashed off dragging the milk float. He went all the way down to the fire station, which was (by road) a good two and half miles from where

he was at the time. The horse was one of those that was fastened onto the fire engine. He got there, apparently, all on his own and everything worked according to plan. To me it was just a fantastic thing, that a horse knew when the maroon went off he had to get to the fire station, and not only that, but because he was a horse that did this sort of journey week after week delivering milk, he knew how to get down there!

We all went to school in Faversham; my brother and I got scholarships to the local Grammar school and we were very happy there. I got into the first eleven for soccer and cricket – I used to be wicket keeper in cricket and usually played right back in the football (soccer) team. I got on very well with my schoolmaster, who also taught mathematics, Mr Hutchinson. There were times when I was growing up that I found being the son of the local policeman wasn't too much fun, and I sometimes found pressures at home a bit too much, and I would go up to see him at Ravenscourt, where they lived, and help him on his allotments. We were always great friends. He also had a load of daughters, including Mollie, Peggy and Pattie who were roughly my age, and his youngest son, John, was a couple of years below me at the Grammar School.

Later my father was moved to Whitstable and there we had the fun of doing sea swimming all the year round. When I was quite young we used to cycle down to Seasalter where I learned to swim. My Uncle Jim used to take me swimming when he came to visit us, and taught a sea swimming stroke (the trudgen, with a flutter kick and crawl arms). Uncle Jim was a swimming bloke for the County and was quite well-known in swimming circles.

Interviews with Imperial Airways

I don't know what inspired me to write to Imperial Airways when I was leaving school, but I did and received a large bundle giving details of the Commercial Trainee scheme and application forms. Reading these over it seemed fascinating to a young bloke who was very much a country bumpkin. I had dreams of going to the Empire and expanding the airlines although I really didn't know what they were doing. In my application form, apart from my headmaster, I was also backed by a gentleman living in Faversham who worked at the Air Ministry in London. It was probably due to him that I got my first interview.

When the due day for the interview came I had to get up to London very early. The only way was to get the first train in the morning that got me to Chatham to get the workman's train. That gave me a very cheap ticket from Faversham to Chatham but then I had to dash out of the train to get a new ticket from Chatham to London, and get back on the same train before it left to go to London to qualify for the workman's fare. But doing it that way I got the fare which was about a quarter of a schoolboy's fare.

Airways Terminal was across the road from platform 1 at Victoria station; it was almost a part of Victoria station. I saw the hall porter and showed him my interview letter, and he sent me indoors to wait, while he reported me upstairs. There was a lounge with a little coffee bar on one side and three long counters where passengers reported. I sat down in one of the settees and looked around but that was when I had a bit of a shock. There was me wearing a Faversham suit, well made, well brushed and well-worn, and looking around seeing one boy in Eton dress, and one in a morning suit, with a top hat even! I realised these were up for interview the same as I was. It made me feel that my chances of getting any further were absolutely nil.

I don't remember anything at all about the interview except being introduced. I gathered there was an Air Commodore there, and a Wing Commander, so when I had the opportunity I mentioned that Major James McCudden (Jimmy) was in our family (second cousin I think it was). He was one of the early air aces in the 1914-18 war and he had more medals than anyone else, I think! After all, I had nothing else to impress these people with, and I came from a country area and although I didn't realise it, I had a country accent! I went home reasonably satisfied with my perfor-mance but realising that I really had no chance with the opposition that was there.

I gathered that there were five hundred people selected for screening and that was just the first screening day. So I just had to go home and get on with living, imagining I couldn't possibly get into Imperial Airways after all, but it had been a good try.

A fortnight later, much to his amazement, Geoffrey received a letter asking him to report to the Institute of Industrial Psychology in London.

That day I did my usual trip using the workman's ticket to get up to London. I found my way to the Institute of Industrial Psychology and met quite a number of fellows - there must have been at least fifty - who were in the same screening group. The Industrial Psychology exams seemed to be stupid, reading things backwards, writing things quickly, all sorts of things. One of the tests involved taking an electric light bulb socket to pieces and sorting it out in numbers and finding you had thirty or forty of each part and when they said "go" you had to assemble them so you had light bulb sockets all ready completed. It really was a bit of a laugh; I really didn't know how to do it till it started, and then rushing to do them in the time, and you get cross-threaded and - what fun everybody had with that!

A Psychologist would recognise these tests for initiative, mental dexterity, methodical approach to an unknown problem and so on. A month later Geoffrey got a letter, anticipating a turn-down. Instead, it was a request to attend another interview at Airways Terminal. He remembered only three people there, and understood from one of the secretaries that this was a very high level interview; the people were some of the most senior people there, including the man in charge of the trainees [McAlpine?] and one of the Air Commodores.

This trainee scheme, it was a paid job, yes, but the pay for the first year was 15 shillings per week [75p], the second year (you got a really big increase) was 30 shillings a week [£1.50], and the third year which was real big stuff, you got 45 shillings a week [£2.25]. Talking it over, my father agreed that he would make up my first and second year to 45 shillings per week, which is what I piously thought I would be able to live on till the third year. I must admit that at that time 45 shillings sounded like an enormous amount of money but I found out you had to do an awful lot of scraping and pinching in order to be able to live on it.

I must have received the offer or the confirmation of getting into the job with great joy and gusto, although I really don't remember much about it. I was taken up to London to a house in Streatham by the parents of a fellow I met while he was holidaying here down in Tankerton; he was Geoffrey Burton, he lived in Beckenham, and his parents had a car. How we got tangled up and they took me up to Streatham and how we got the idea of the digs in Streatham I can't remember at all. But on 23rd Sept 1933, I duly reported to Imperial Airways at Airways Terminal as the most junior of all the people in all the official ranks, namely first year commercial trainee.

Chapter 2:
Commercial Trainee

Class of 1933

Starting out in a new job, and in the big city, was a big step for Geoffrey. He was very much in awe of everything around him. Imperial Airways was an organisation with a tremendous reputation, and it impressed him considerably. Geoffrey had the right attitude, even for a very naive eighteen-year-old.

I tried very hard to be a good lad, to do as I was told and behave myself properly.

I remember the first day when all seven of us, five from the UK and two from overseas, met up for the first time. There was Douglas Grey, nephew of Lord Grey; Ian Scott-Hill who apparently was again very well known (well, his family was); John Maspero who lived in the Channel Islands; Ross Stainton who many years later became chairman of BOAC, (created from Imperial Airways) and myself, an utter nobody. And the overseas boys, both from India, were Sunny Sunduram and H A Durawala.

Geoffrey lost touch with Sunny Sunduram but they met again in the early 50s working for the International Air Traffic Agency, as it was called then, IATA in Montreal.

So that first day I remember we assembled in the office of the General Services Manager - that was his official title, actually it was the Air Commodore [Fletcher] - all standing round his desk and he gave us a lecture. What really stays in my mind about that was his emphasis on loyalty not just to each other but to the company. In fact his pay-off line was "and your first duty is to the Company, your second duty is to the Company and your third duty is to the Company"!

This loyalty to Imperial Airways was a thing that grew on you because it was all around you. It was noticeable that all the employees, even the secretaries and the junior girls, they all had this particular loyalty to the airline - it was something that not only built up the airline itself but made all the staff feel as though they were in one big family.

Orientation

The Air Commodore told us what was allocated to each of us. The basic programme was three months in every branch of the organisation. We were supposed to learn as much as we possibly could, get an idea of how all the parts of the airline ran and how they were co-ordinated to produce the final product. I was first allocated to the Traffic Manager. The Traffic Manager then was, I suppose, the boss of all the field staff, not flying or engineering, but all the other parts of the organisation. He had to help him a fellow called James Latte [Matthey?] famous for always using green ink. And another fellow he had, a totally different category, was Anthony Downing.

The Traffic Manager, Denis Handover, had as his secretary then Sheila Tracy, who many years later as Sheila Porch was the Public Relations manager of BOAC. I found Sheila most helpful and cooperative. She seemed to me a highly educated and very sophisticated woman, where I was poorly educated and very much a country cousin up into a world that was totally alien to him; she helped very much with hints etc., but equally Anthony Downing also helped me settle in to the type of life I was going to live. He had, I think, propensities toward the stage, to acting and that sort of thing. He was a delightful fellow and although he was nowhere near the standard of efficiency of James Latte he was helpful, he gave hints and guided me for quite a while when I was getting into the swing of being an employee.

Charts

As a commercial trainee we were expected to learn fast, to get on and do the job and be one who would ultimately become somebody in the senior ranks of the organisation. I don't remember all that I had to do while I was working in that position but one thing was that always at 9 am you had to take the Charts up to the Managing Director. Now the Charts were a placing on a great big piece of graph paper of all the flights of the Airways as at the previous closedown of operations [there was normally no night flying]. They were just really coloured lines placed on a chart down to various parts of the world, giving their times of arrival and departure and, if anything had gone wrong, an indication of what had gone wrong and this sort of thing. It was, however, necessary for you, as a junior presenting these to the Managing Director, to have a fairly good idea of what the position was of the fleet otherwise the Managing Director would ask you question and you could either shiver in your shoes or you came out and gave him a proper answer. He was of course the top man and one obviously did one's best in order to keep in his good books.

Sports & Social Club

I enjoyed working up there at Airways Terminal. At that time they were still organising things and one of the things they were organising was the Imperial Airways Sports & Social Club. Although the Social Club never really (in my time) got going, the Sports Club seemed to develop – it started basically with the swimming session. We used to have sessions with the local clubs, and we didn't have to pay the usual fee, we paid a club membership fee only, very much cheaper than if we were going on our own. We also organised ourselves into teams and subsequently did competitions between various swimming clubs who were around in the London area. I remember that the principal swimmer that used to compete was a young fellow in the Publicity Dept, and the other was Ross Stainton who was a very good swimmer. Dick Cole also a good swimmer and Bill Daintree – both recruited as trainees the year previously but based on the Red Sea Gulf down by Port Suez. Amongst the women swimmers there was Sheila Tracy, she was very good, and two girls that were in the telephone exchange. One was Miss Russell, and her junior subsequently married Len Rashbrook, her name was Jean.

I was fortunately fairly highly rated within the Swimming Club. With the help of their coach, I was also able to develop a proper crawl as opposed to the trudgen, which I used because that was by the far the best thing to use in sea with waves.

I qualified in the Airways swimming club to represent them in the relay and I still have a half pint pewter pot with a glass bottom which was the prize one year for the members of the winning relay team! I was also young enough and probably stupid enough to get myself talked into being a member of the soccer team for Airways at London. We used to play football against all sorts of teams, usually out of town, which meant travelling a bit and obviously paying for it, and I couldn't afford much expenditure on the income I was getting. Although my father had agreed to make up my pay to 45 shillings a week, I had to pay National Insurance 1s 2d, which made a lot of difference, that was a lot of money out of 15s. But when I was working down on the passenger counter, I met some of the lads who introduced me to the Southern Railways Porters Club.

This club is for the Southern Railway porters in Victoria station; it was open to the Airways junior people and I was able to join for one shilling a year membership fee. But when one was working on shifts, you could go over to the SRP club and get a jolly good breakfast, which would usually consist of at least bacon, fried bread, fried egg, cup of coffee and something else - I don't know what now, but a good substantial meal and it only cost you a shilling! And this used to set me up for a whole day.

Meteorology

We appeared to shift jobs every three months. Three months at Victoria were followed by three months at Croydon, and occasionally you might do three months up in the West End on the sales counters, but usually we were at the terminal at Victoria or Croydon. The most boring of those jobs was in Accounts, and although I suppose it did me good to know how the accounts were run, and the department organised, and what various parts of the accounts organisation covered what, nevertheless I did find it a bore and was happy when my three months there were over.

On one occasion when I was down working in Export department, which was very interesting, I was also doing a meteorological (Met) course.

Twice a week I had to go up to the Met Office at Croydon airport control tower, where I was initially given talks about clouds, weather generally, winds and so on, and subsequently I was taken up on the roof and shown how to take readings for the upper winds and how to do the calculations. This was quite fun, especially as my stint happened in the summer time! If it had been winter, it wouldn't have been any fun at all because you were standing right up on the top of the control tower, bleak, open to the weather on all sides. The weather balloon was filled with hydrogen but carried a weight so you knew how many feet per second it rose in the atmosphere. You sent up your balloon; then, by watching it through a complicated theodolite type of telescope, winding little handles there and little handles somewhere else, at special time intervals you read the figures on three of the angles. You went on

timing it and reading the figures until you lost your balloon or it disappeared. Usually, of course, with cloud around you lost it through the cloud at fairly low altitude but on one particular occasion I was very lucky, I thought myself marvellous, because I took right it up to 35,000 feet and I was watching it when it burst. Apparently that had been the highest that any of the trainee boys had ever taken the balloon up. The problem, though, was that because I'd taken it up so far I had to do even more calculations than usual, to produce a table showing what the winds were at every 500 feet all the way up to 35,000! It took me a long, long time with my slide rule to work that one out.

Although I was very pleased to make this very high observation it really was rather academic. In those days, the absolute highest a plane would fly would be 9,000 feet because above that height (well, 10,000 ft) oxygen had to be available to all crew and passengers. So the normal operating height was between 2,500 and 6,000, 7,000 feet at the most. But I enjoyed the course that I did with the Met Office people at Croydon airport. Apart from the fact that I enjoyed the work, it came in terribly useful later on when I was down in bush stations in Africa. There was no one there who knew anything about the weather apart from what it was doing on the ground, and I found I had to report to the main weather stations of each country I was in. Each morning at a certain time I would have to report to wherever the Centre was, so Nairobi or Port Bell or Khartoum or Dar Es Salaam, to give them a report of the weather to a certain formula. The formula was one that could be signalled in a ten letter code group and it meant that somebody could give the weather officials actual weathers and they could draw up their synoptic charts and make their forecasts.

The thing I found most difficult was being able to estimate the height of cloud. You haven't anywhere you can go and measure them and only from doing some balloon work on measuring when it disappeared gave me some idea of where the cloud was located and what it looked like at different altitudes. Anyway, I enjoyed the course and it came in jolly useful for quite a number of years when I was in Africa.

Le Touquet

Many other things happened during training – little incidents like when I went out to Le Touquet with Alfie Pigg. He was an experienced Traffic Clerk in Croydon at the time, and he was sent over, with me to help him, to open up operations at this fashionable resort for 'the season'. It was really only a short period - I think I was only over there for a fortnight - but because of the importance to the airline, to have operations into and out of Le Touquet at that period, well, we did our stuff and I enjoyed it thoroughly. We had to spend a lot of hours in the office. Apart from daytime business, many of the passengers were people using the casinos and the gaming tables. They would come out about 4 o'clock, 5 o'clock in the morning, and want to go home later on that day. If we weren't available to see what the state of the bookings was and to do what was necessary with them, they'd have got very browned off with Imperial Airways. Part of the training was, whatever you did, you saw that no passenger got mad at the airline; he always had to be treated so the airline came out well and the passenger always thought highly of the airline.

Apart from enjoying that trip, it was probably the first time in my life I stayed in a really top class hotel. The one we stayed at in Le Touquet was called Le Normandie and it really was an attractive place. I learned a lot too, and it was just as well that I had Alfie Pigg with me. He was a youngish lad, but he was older than me and he had his head screwed on sensibly. He taught me how to behave and how to act and how to, well, exist, in the hotel life of a much higher standard than I was used to.

Geoffrey met Alfie Pigg occasionally during his working life but got to know him well when they met at Harefield Hospital on a heart clinic day. Both had heart trouble, and Alfie was further advanced in his recovery than Geoffrey at that time. "He certainly helped me adjust mentally to getting over my heart problems. His help, talking to me and explaining things and how they could happen and how he'd met them, was a great help to me, as he had been when I was much, much younger, working down at Croydon with him."

Another time that stands out in my mind was when I was working with the General Sales Manager at Victoria. I was called into his office, and there he was on his hands and knees! Well, he was Air Commodore, but you don't expect him to be on his hands and knees. He had a great big map there and he said: "Come and play bears with me and show me where Homs is!" It was then I realised we had a plane that had diverted and gone down at some sort of emergency landing strip. The report had indicated 'Homs' but it hadn't indicated which country Homs was in, nor had it given any latitude or longitude. By studying it we found three areas of Homs; around the North African coast, the Lebanese coast and inland in Lebanon. Three places, and we could only guess from the course the plane should have been on which was which. He was very pleased when we found it on the map.

Lodgings and commuting

I originally came up to Airways Terminal (where the office was) from Streatham on the tram. It was a long journey and it wasn't really a comfortable one, and in wintertime it was very cold but with the tram you could get a one shilling all-day ticket and you could travel anywhere that the tram operated south of the river [Thames]. So I could get up to London and back again for a shilling, then I only had a three pence bus fare from Vauxhall Bridge up to Victoria station.

Later on when I got myself established I got my bike up to my digs and I used to cycle up from Streatham to Victoria. It was a tricky trip with all the cabs on the roads and the rest of the traffic; nowhere as bad as these days, but it *was* tricky and the road could be slippery. I remember one time it was wet and I turned a corner and completely skidded across the road. I completely ruined the mackintosh I was wearing, which I could ill afford because to replace that would cost me a large proportion of my weekly allowance.

At one time during my training at Croydon in 1934 or 35 I came back up to Victoria and found some digs in St George's Street up in about the 3rd or 4th floor. I found we had some other Airways people in there. We had Davidge Pitts and Denis Lloyd and also a painter fellow, I can't remember his name. The painter had recently been over to Germany and had been very full of the German Youth and the discipline and all that. I subsequently met Davidge Pitts down at Croydon. It used to be pretty embarrassing: because of my name Pett, I used to get a lot of his telephone calls. It was usually an irate young lady fed up because she'd turned up for a date with him and he'd never arrived, so she wanted to sort things out. It got me into an awful lot of trouble - I had a terrible job trying to convince them that I was Geoffrey Pett and nothing at all to do with Davidge Pitts.

Denis Lloyd was a South African, I didn't meet him again until Lindi in 1937, when he came up from South Africa in order to take over the Lindi station.

The four of us in the lodgings in St George's Street were all pretty broke and we had to look after our money the best we could. Very frequently we got to Thursday evening [payday would be each Friday] and it was a case of finding out who had got any gas in their gas stove - you had to put money in your gas meter like you had to for your electric heater - which was the only thing that would also heat a kettle. We even got to the stage of sharing out the money we had in our pockets so one of us could go down the delicatessen to get something to eat for an evening meal between us. I had an advantage with my breakfast from the Porters Club, but if I was working very early in the morning I'd get a breakfast allowance of about 2/6 [2s 6d or 12.5 pence] which meant if I had breakfast in the Porters Club I had 1/6 left for any meals later that day.

Avro crash

An incident occurred that gave me insight and a certain amount of experience.

We had one aircraft reported to have crashed in northern France, it was an Avro-10 I think; if I remember rightly it hit a rock pile and went down in bad weather. There were only crew on board, I don't think there were any passengers at all, but that didn't make any difference; an aircraft had crashed and the emergency drill was automatically put in and I realised then that there was a lot of feeling amongst the staff involved that *we* had had a crash, and it really was *we*, it wasn't anything to do with the pilot or the crew, or the aircraft or the engineering – it was we, our airplane, our airline, and we had to do something and stand by to look after our aeroplane.

This particular situation was very difficult as one of the secretaries was engaged to the pilot, and until we got all the full report of the crash with the details of bodies, it really was very embarrassing. I found it particularly embarrassing as I was the youngest around the place and hadn't experienced that before. I had no idea how to cope with or react to people's emotions.

Chapter 3:
Brindisi

Routes to Italy

In October 1935 Geoffrey had done most of the departments around the UK and was due for training session in Europe. Now aged twenty, he was posted to Brindisi in the south of Italy, the point where the Scipio class flying boats took over from land transport and carried passengers across to Alexandria.

Here I had some luck because at that time Imperial Airways were thinking of operating a land plane through to Brindisi. They didn't have permission to fly a land route through Paris to Rome. The 'freedoms of the air' were very, very restricted in those days and it meant that Imperial Airways weren't able to fly our passengers over Italy. For that reason we had to put our passengers on a train at Paris and take them by train to Brindisi and fly them out of Italy on a flying boat. In view of the possibility of rights being granted they were planning an airline across, and we had some new airplanes called the Avro-19. These were used in the war as the Anson, but I was sent out on the first of the Anson flights down to Brindisi, on G-ACRN.

The skipper was Dudley Travers, who was quite a senior bloke, even in those days. After we left Marseille where we'd stayed the first night, we were flying on to Rome, but the cloud came down. Poor old Dudley Travers, he really didn't know what was going on and couldn't get any radio contact, and the shouting that was going on about what to do and where to go! You had to shout of course because the noise in the cockpit was rather high. I was very fortunate because I was able to break in and tell him that if he flew down the coast and found the pylons running north-east he could follow those and it would lead him to a new aerodrome. It had only been open a short time - Fiumicino.

He looked at me and asked, "how do you know about it?"

"I've been working with Air Commodore Brackley. The

routing came up when they were planning this way into Fiumicino."

"Well, I don't know anything about it, it's not marked on my charts."

Anyway, he took a chance and we flew down the coast a bit and found the pylons, and he turned and flew in, and we landed in Fiumicino.

It was a tiny little aerodrome; this so-called new one was more of a stadium, with central area and around it banks and banks of seats. You could just think of it as a football stadium. Landing in there was quite tricky to say the least. We had to come in very steeply then you were rolling fast and we had to turn very rapidly to avoid running into the seating at the other end. Then we swung round and dug our nearside wingtip into the grass – altogether it was quite a hairy landing! But it didn't damage the aircraft and we were able to get away later on that afternoon.

Life in Brindisi

Brindisi: we all stayed in the Albergo Internationale, which was really the only hotel, the rest were just fleapits. It was right down on the quayside, which was where the boats tied up and discharged passengers, but also the freighters tied up and you had the noise of the cranes loading and unloading, which was usually in the middle of the night. But it wasn't too bad, and the passenger frequency wasn't that great. I was lucky insofar as I had a room up on the third floor with a tiny balcony overlooking the harbour, which meant I had a nice view and plenty of air - the fact that I had certain odours coming up from the outside was just one of those things.

Round there the principal form of transport was the horse and cart, the carozza, which was for a couple of passengers, at most four. I don't know how you'd describe a carozza – it was the principal transport. There weren't any motorised taxis or cabs, not that I remember anyway; in the town you just called for a carozza. Anyway as there was the equivalent of a taxi station for about three of these carozza outside the hotel, the odour drifting up from below of horse urine.

Next to the main entrance of the hotel there was an equivalent of a hole-in-the-wall, which was the local bar. I suppose to a large extent it was the bar available for staff off the boats, but for us it was a reasonable place to go. It was far cheaper than the wine in the hotel and at the same time it taught us something about the local wines and the local brews, and we were able to get some sort of conversation with the locals, although they were not the 'higher grade' Italians that people would normally think about. It was in there that we used to buy our Italian cigarettes. They were the nationalised industry ones called Tres Stilbe, and one of the fellows there used to get his cigars, well they weren't really cigars they were long thin wrapped leaves of tobacco, cheroots.

Information gathering

There was a passenger who was a regular between Alexandria and London that we all got very pally with and he used to use our common room. On one occasion I got talking to him and he asked me about a photograph that he'd had from me earlier of an ordinary cargo vessel. I'd given him the photograph because it seemed to have the most peculiar deck cargo and I didn't know what it was, and although I didn't really care it seemed odd to me, and he seemed to be interested. On this particular occasion, he asked me where I got the photos developed.

"Oh the usual, the local photography bloke," I said,

"Have you got the negative?"

"Well, yes."

"Well, I think it would be unwise of you to keep it," he said, "but on the other hand, I would rather like to have it. I showed the picture to the intelligence people in Alexandria."

They had discovered there was a large area off the coast of Eritrea and Abyssinia that was mined, and they were wondering how they had got there. The photograph he had shown them seemed to show the ship taking them out to the Red Sea. When they'd done their stuff with the photograph, they discovered the cargo that I didn't know anything about was a deck cargo of mines. So he suggested to me that if I got rid of that negative, if anyone started asking any questions at least that wouldn't be any evidence against me.

It was only then that I cottoned on to the fact that he was either with naval or military intelligence and in fact what I really was doing was spying on the Italians on behalf of the British Government. It was so easy to talk to this guy about what I'd seen that I really was passing on what became military intelligence.

Then there was the occasion when during the night a number of Italian battleships moved into Brindisi harbour and anchored out there. As we had a 'boat coming in that afternoon it was necessary to let them know about it. So we transmitted a message to Alexandria, telling them that there were these battleships in the harbour. We had a grid reference of the harbour and we were able to say what grid these battleships were anchored in so the skipper of the flying boat had a reasonable idea of what it would be like looking down at the harbour. This was particularly important if he was coming in late and we had to put a night landing flare out for him. But on that occasion when I mentioned it to this regular passenger, he said, "yes, I knew there were going to be these ships in the harbour. I'd be very interested if you happened to know the names of the ships."

Even then, at that time, I didn't realise what was going on; in fact, the whole thing really didn't come to a head in my own mind until 1942 when I was up in Alexandria having discussions at some branch of the Headquarters of Middle East forces. Someone was talking about the possibility of an attack on Southern Italy and they mentioned Brindisi.

I hesitatingly asked, "have you got any info about Brindisi?"

The fellow said, "yes, we've got quite a bit of information but it's all been recorded as third class."

"What do you mean by third class?"

"Well, it's information that was collected over the years from some Britishers that happened to be based in Brindisi and from what they observed we got information and we gleaned it and we've been able to get a fair idea of what the problems and position is around there."

"What sort of problems and positions?"

"Well, we had the information about the position of coastal guns which was very useful; apparently they used to sail around the harbour quite a bit and a fellow noticed these guns and mentioned it to one of our people. And another one seemed to indicate that all sorts of anti-aircraft guns were all around in various places, some of which were hidden under grass mounds; when they wanted to exercise them the whole mound was lifted up and the guns were revealed underneath. So, you know, we have reasonable information, but we don't know how exact or accurate it is because of course, these were ordinary civilians and they had no training for getting that sort of information."

And it was really only then I realised that the ships and the names of guns, the batteries and the coastal batteries, this information had all been collected by various Airways people, and the anti-aircraft guns, this was 'gleaned' on the cycle rides going out in the countryside. And you know, we never knew that the other was doing that; I gather that Stephen Broad was the one that was doing comments and reports on the coastal gun emplacements, but I never knew this at all. It was only when I was talking to Headquarters Middle East in 1942 that this really came out. It shows how easy it is for an ordinary civilian to fall into a trap of spying without realising what he's doing, but just being a matter of interest to this courier bloke who was going on between Alexandria and London.

Passenger handling

Part of the job in Brindisi was meeting the passengers on the train. We, Imperial Airways, weren't allowed to fly over Italy and our passengers were flown from London to Paris and they were put on the train and went right the way through to Brindisi where they arrived at 3.30 in the morning, a beautiful time wasn't it? There we met the train, well it was the terminus anyway, and we arranged for our passengers, their baggage, and the mail, which was also on the train, to be transferred to our flying boat. Of course we took the passengers into the hotel so they could have a reasonable stretch and breakfast and washrooms et cetera, while we were sorting out the baggage and the mail and checking that over, not only with the mail people from the train but picking up the local mail too. We'd take it across in the launch to the customs people and get it loaded onto the flying boat.

Of course, the flying boats in those days we were principally using were the three Scipio class, well we used to call the Scipio class, a four engine Short flying boat. I don't know how many passengers they carried but they operated for many years between there and Alexandria. In those days, we thought them a thoroughly beautiful aircraft.

It was strange though, meeting these passengers at Brindisi railway station, because you could be caught up in a tangle of the conductor speaking French, the porters and railway staff speaking Italian, and the passengers speaking English or French or Italian. So you finished up automatically talking back to where the sound came from in the language the sound was. You didn't think whether you were talking in Italian or French or English, you were just replying to the sound that you had picked up. It was quite interesting because it was not until then that I cottoned onto the idea that if you want to learn a language, you have to have the sound of it first before you can have any real idea of learning it.

I came home from Brindisi in early August 1936. Having finished my three-year training period, I was now hoping I would be taken on as a permanent member of staff. I came home by the usual route of those days, the train through to Paris and then flying from Paris to Croydon, and reported in at Airways Terminal; I was told I was now due for six weeks leave, before reporting for overseas duty. I would get a letter from them telling me when I ought to report at the end of my leave, and to go off and thoroughly enjoy myself! So that, I suppose, really brought the first phase of my life in Airways to an end.

Chapter 4:
Centaurus

This chapter contains what is to me one of the most fascinating tales, the testing of the flying boat Centaurus, *before Imperial Airways took it over from the manufacturers, Shorts. The first official trip, which collected the Christmas mail, is also mentioned in one of the other Flying Boat books.*

Although my father had retired he was still in Tankerton, Kent and so I spent most of that time down in Tankerton and with the crowd I'd made friends with earlier, centred on the swimming club. The hub of the gang down there was the Sanders family, Brian was the second son and the daughter was Joan. We subsequently met up again in the late 1980s when she and her husband were living in Mudeford in Hampshire. The swimming club had a hut in Tankerton that was almost next to the hut the Sanders family had, which was the reason why we centred round them. Toward the end of the holiday, John Ingram's mother decided to let us know that she was selling the bungalow they were living in and emigrating to New Zealand. He subsequently left; we corresponded while he was in New Zealand and he later became manager of one of the big departmental stores there. We still kept in touch when he was on the island of Raratonga up in the Cook Group. There was also Barry Gregory: towards the end of my holiday he contracted polio and unfortunately he died.

One day we were on the beach, strolling along the promenade down by the beach and we saw a couple of girls walking towards us in the other direction. I thought that's funny, that one looks familiar. I realised she was the junior office girl attached to the Met Office at Croydon, Margaret Breeze. As I'd passed her and acknowledged her in the Met Office (I hadn't really said anything to her) I decided I'd speak to her then, and found that she and her girlfriend were on holiday down in Whitstable for a fortnight. So I invited them along to join our crowd on the beach, and they spent quite a number of hours with the crowd. They seemed to enjoy themselves, so when I went back up to London I was able to keep in touch. We did meet several times and I enjoyed her company; that was Met Office Peggy, sometimes known as the Cold Front or the Iceberg, depending I suppose for what the relations with the various boys were with Peggy of the Met Office!

I returned to work after the holiday in the end of August 1936 and after a bit of mucking about, I was told to report down to Shorts at Rochester where I was being attached nominally as Purser to the flying boat that was being built there.

Acceptance tests

I went down and reported to the skipper of the new flying boat, Captain Egglesfield. I made contact with him at the Bull Hotel in Rochester, because that was where the crew was living. The crew of *Centaurus* consisted of Egglesfield, Carlos Madge the first officer, Paddy Coussans the radio officer who also did pick up of moorings etc. There was a fellow called Phillips, either an Australian or a New Zealander, who was the steward, and then myself as the Purser.

My job covered just about everything except the technical side; learning the problems of loading it and trimming it, also checking equipment that was supplied under contract by the Shorts people, and carrying out all sorts of tests that the skipper wanted me to do on his behalf. We were doing the acceptance tests for the aircraft for Imperial Airways and until it was cleared by the aircrew as being acceptable, the aircraft remained the property of Shorts and was not taken over by Imperial Airways.

Centaurus, G-ADUT, was the second, well third, of the C class flying boats. While I was there ADHL, *Canopus*, finished its acceptance test and flew off accepted by Imperial Airways. Then there was ADUU, which was *Cavalier*, that was there, crated, because it was to be loaded onto ship, taken across the Atlantic and rebuilt to operate the New York – Bermuda flights. Imperial Airways were then exploiting them because of certain 'difficult attitudes' by the Americans over the possibility of transatlantic flight.

Loading, stowing and trim

Apart from the technical side of trim on the aircraft for which I was responsible, I had to see the equipment being loaded, check off whether the right number of saucers and cups and spoons and blankets and rugs. Oh yes, there were blankets, because that C class flying boat, the S23 when it was named by Imperial Airways, it was supposed to be equipped with eight bunks with all their necessary sheets and blankets and pillows and pillowcases. This equipment was all stored up in the centre section of the wing across the top of the flying boat body, and it was jolly difficult to get it up there and properly loaded, but how it was ever going to be used on a trip I don't quite know. Although we did carry out on three occasions the equipping of the flying boat with all eight bunks. There were four in the centre cabins and four in the nose cabins. There were none in the main rear cabin at all.

Actually, I thoroughly enjoyed it at Rochester - apart from the fact we used to go down there first thing in the morning, rain or shine, blow or hail, on the basis that we might be taking off and doing more stress tests. I had a lot of fun with their stress people because as it was still Shorts' property I had to get their formal approval for the loading of the aircraft - that it was correctly trimmed for flight - before we could take off. Now I'd been reasonably used to the trim of various aircraft, not only at Croydon, but also various Shorts boats such as the Scipio boats down in Brindisi, so it didn't haze (sic) me too much. The calculation of the centre of gravity used a certain amount of maths that I was reasonably familiar with because it tied up with the maths that I'd done at school.

On one particular evening, we got a signal from headquarters: the spare engine that we had loaded in the flying boat they wanted urgently somewhere else, so they were taking it out and shipping it off. The engineering side did that during the night. But the next morning, before we could get flying, the aircraft had to be checked because the removal of the engine from the rear hold meant the centre of gravity was all out. Well, I went up to the stress office of Shorts and brought my papers up to them and said to the fellow in charge I thought if we moved this bit of this and that bit of that back into the rear hold then that would be all right. He said "Oh you can't do that sort of thing!" Out came a great piece of paper and we started off with the weight empty, the aircraft with how much fuel there was in and how the moment moved and the weight of the captain and each member of the crew and the weight of the pantry and everything. We went all over it, all the moveable items, which meant we ended up with two sheets of foolscap (which is the usual drill, you see, up in the Stress Office) completed line by line to finish up at the end with a trim, which showed that if we moved just about 300 kilos from our forward upper hold into the rear hold it would bring the centre of gravity back within the gravity range.

The poor old stress bloke in Shorts said, "I can't understand you people, how do you just work it out that you just move that? You do it in your head without doing it properly, and you come out right all the time!"

Altitude test

There was the day when Egglesfield was doing takeoff tests, and for this particular one we were told we were doing altitude. The skipper wanted to find out how it behaved at different altitudes and amongst other things we just went climbing and climbing, and climbing! And we got colder and colder and colder and tireder and tireder partly because of lack of oxygen – we had no oxygen at all – and the aircraft eventually couldn't go any more and I think to some extent Captain Egglesfield couldn't cope with trying to fly the thing at 21,000 feet, which in those days was a helluva height! And with no oxygen as well! We were all very pleased when we came down slowly, slowly and eventually touched down in Rochester.

There was also the tricky business of flying out of Rochester, because it's not a very long straight stretch of the river Medway. Coming in over Rochester bridge, past the castle and down on the water beside the Shorts works was a tricky business. If you got side winds, cross winds, blowing, it was very difficult work on the rudder to keep the 'boat coming down the river.

Another day, after we'd taken off, I was standing up in the cockpit with the skipper and first officer. Egglesfield asked me if I would go back into the rear hold, as far back as I could, and wait there - contrary to all the rules, of course - and wait there until we'd tied up, because he wanted to know what the reactions were right back in the tail section during landings. As there were no handholds at all, I just had to grab lashing points where they were or the strings or framework within the tail section, it was a pretty hairy thing to do. Standing around there with the tail coming from left to right and up and down, but mostly it was side slipping... I didn't like it at all – it was horrible!

Christmas mail

The great day dawned when Imperial Airways officially accepted *Centaurus* and we were instructed to deliver it to Alexandria. Now the skipper planned to fly from Rochester down to Bordeaux, Bordeaux-Marseilles, Marseilles-Rome etc., but the morning we were due to leave we had a signal to say we were to go into Southampton.

There we found we were due to take on part of the Christmas mail that had already accumulated to take onward to Alexandria for distribution to the Far East and South Africa. It was quite fun landing in Southampton because it was the first time we'd done a night landing in the flying boat, but you know, Egglesfield was such a good pilot he could do that sort of thing with no trouble at all. We eventually moored and had this barge come alongside, it was a motorboat really, and who was on board but our Traffic Director, Denis Handover. He was there with this mail and a couple of other fellows and a couple of loaders and they proceeded to load the mail and I had to organise the loading system because they hadn't signalled me in advance telling me what load it was. I hadn't been instructed on the forerunner of the Christmas mail peak loads. We got it all loaded, but the strange thing was, here I'd got the Traffic Director, slinging mailbags into the aircraft while I was seeing where they were put!

Southampton to Alexandria

We left the next morning from Southampton and went from there down to Bordeaux, Bordeaux to Marseilles, Marseilles down to Lake Vechiano which was again a new place for landing at Rome. Then from there down to Brindisi, then from Brindisi down to Athens. We night stopped in Marseilles on the first night and on the second one in Athens. I remember that, because during the night something happened.

During the night the local police came demanding passports of the crew and I made up I hadn't got them because I didn't want them to lose them, and finished up by agreeing that I would produce the passports the following morning down at the port before we left. That seemed to quieten things down but in the morning, I discovered that the steward and the flight engineer (because we had a flight engineer on our way out), they had 'sampled' the delights of Athens rather too much and the local police had picked them up. I had earlier been out with the crew, because the skipper had said let's go and have a drink in the town, so I had joined them. Quite honestly I'd had more than I'd wanted to, even leaving early. We got them away all right, but the trip the following morning down from Athens was through Souda Bay in Crete then down to Alexandria, and we were flying into a headwind all the way of about thirty miles an hour. The skipper decided he was going to fly low, and flying low means we bounce like mad, and it seemed almost like the waves were coming up and slapping the bottom of the flying boat. I didn't enjoy the trip because of my head, but how the poor old steward and flight engineer coped I just don't know because they really did take on a load that previous night!

I don't really remember what happened after arriving at Alexandria except I finished off my report and gave it to the station superintendant or the area manager for forwarding to the Traffic Manager. This report was supposed to be information from which they would draw up the Rules and Guidance for Pursers, who were being created as a new job and new vacancy with the introduction of the C Class flying boats. The duties of the Pursers were not defined in any way and as a result of my report and also that of Clive Adams who had come out on *Canopus*, a month or so earlier, I gathered the two reports would be scrutinised and the rules and responsibilities of the Purser would be promulgated. I never really heard anything about it, no one said thanks for your report and I didn't see any instructions issued. The title Purser seemed to disappear very quickly and they just became flight clerks. Anyway, I left *Centaurus* and carried on down to Central Africa.

Chapter 5:
Nairobi

It's late 1936, Geoffrey is twenty-one years old, and he's on his own in Africa. Admittedly he's got orders for where to report, and people flying aeroplanes to get advice from, but he's basically now on his own, and upholding the honour of Imperial Airways as he's been trained to do.

Alexandria to Kisumu

All I remember of the trip down from Alexandria was that we were approaching Juba in the Hannibal, which was the overseas version of the Heracles HP42, and we had trouble in landing at Juba because there was a bush fire raging. We had to circle around until the fire had passed over the airport; the airport runway was all grass anyway, and we needed the grass and foliage to cool down sufficiently so that our tyres wouldn't burst on contact with the ashes. It was a very interesting trip. As we circled around you could see all these animals running in front of this bush fire, which was spreading down from the northeast to the southwest. It seemed to rush along, and the poor animals - the only ones I didn't see were elephant and giraffe - all the smaller type of animals including rhinos were just rushing to get out of the way of these flames.

The area headquarters, where I had to report, were at Nairobi. I got down to Kisumu and there I found there was no way of getting over to Nairobi for a week or so, unless I got a lift with a fellow who had been on leave in Kisumu and was going back to Nairobi. I didn't know the country and didn't know the people so I thought jolly good, and why not? So I got in touch with this fellow and we left the next morning. I dumped my bags in the back, because he had a Ford truck, not a car, and I got in the cab with him and off we went. I hadn't realised what sort of country it was between Kisumu and Nairobi, and I'd forgotten that the area is 5,000 or 6,000 feet above sea level, so that after we'd left Kisumu we started climbing out of the Rift Valley. I'd never heard of the Rift Valley in those days and didn't know what it was, but we were certainly climbing up, it was beautiful countryside but it was getting colder and colder and I found we had frost on the ground around us. It was fortunate that the cab of the truck was reasonably warm!

At one time, the fellow driving said, "Ah well, the engine's warm enough now so we can switch over."

"What do you mean, switch over?"

"Well, paraffin here's so much cheaper than petrol that when you can, you run on paraffin. So now the engine's nice and warm I'm going to switch over to my auxiliary tank which is paraffin."

And from then on we ran on paraffin, although it was supposed to be a petrol engine.

Life in Nairobi, 1937

The only thing I remember about my arrival in Nairobi is that I stayed in the Avenue Hotel. I must have arrived in Nairobi between the 20th and 23rd December 1936. It was a day or two later that the King's Speech came on at the equivalent of 3 o'clock in the afternoon. It was the custom in my family to stand, so I stood up when the King was announced, and I noticed that other people in the room slowly got to their feet and so everyone in the room was standing during the King's Speech.

After a short while at the Avenue Hotel, I moved out to the Hill Hotel, which was on the way out to the airport. The airport in those days was just a green grass patch with a couple of hangars and, apart from Imperial Airways operating through there, it was also the base for Wilson Airways and the Wilson Flying Club. Wilson Airways subsequently grew and became a very important member of the air transport routes. The Hill Hotel as I remember was a very charming place. We had our own rooms on a long stretch going away from the hotel into the countryside, trees and shrubs. The rooms were very pleasant indeed, and the food; we lived on a half board basis, breakfast and dinner, and if we wanted lunch anywhere we got our own. This suited us very well when we were working around and we could always get something in Nairobi Town.

Also in the Hill Hotel were two couples who were influenced me quite a bit and introduced me to life in the Colonies. They were Stanley White and his wife, and the Manning brothers.

The Manning brothers, one worked for Wilson Airways and the other was working for the Government in survey work. The other couple really introduced me to social living in the Nairobi area. They used to invite me out when they went to hotel get-togethers and to evenings at Hoares, which was the liveliest hotel in town. I went along on blind dates because they had friends, female friends, who were looking for tall partners. Nothing romantic about it or anything like that, it was just a friendly arrangement and it did me good because it brought me out into the social life of a town, like Nairobi was in those days. The association with the Manning brothers was a different type altogether. They had a Ford V8 truck and they used to go up country out of Nairobi quite a bit together. Both of them were born and bred in Kenya and they used to go up into the bush, just looking at animals; there was no question of shooting them or anything like that but they were just interested in their own home country. As a result they introduced me into the life of being interested in nature and the natural history of Kenya. I owe them a great deal of thanks; their introduction to the bush and how to behave in order to look after yourself, and to see and protect yourself from animals without the use of guns, set me up and gave me a lot of amusement throughout the rest of my life in Africa.

Stanley White also introduced me to golf. He was a keen golfer and liked to play the game occasionally. He suggested I came along with him on one occasion, and I walked around a lovely golf course that was in Nairobi, and I thought, well, I might as well try to do something about it. So I went to the Indian dookas behind the main street in Nairobi and eventually picked up a bag with about five clubs in it, for about £2, I suppose, wooden shafted clubs because that was the sort of thing one had then. There was a driver and a spoon, and three other clubs, so it was enough for me to knock a little white ball around. I had those for years; they travelled around with me until I went up to Cairo. I never really got interested in golf, but it was a nice place to go. Wherever I was, if you went along to the golf course you found the most attractive part of the countryside and the only place you could reasonably walk and enjoy yourself. One I returned to after I'd been in the Sudan for a couple of years was down at Brackenhurst, which was outside Nairobi. It really was the most beautiful area and to come from where I'd been in the Sudan to a wonderful country, green and lovely sunshine, warm, dew on the cobwebs on the trees, walking around the fairway with the shrubs and bushes around, it was delightful. I would never have found it if it hadn't been for the fact I'd got this cheap bag of golf clubs from the Indian dooka in Nairobi.

A hotel that Stanley White and his wife introduced me to for a social evening was the Norfolk Hotel. The Norfolk epitomised to me the hotel living of Colonial Africa. It really was a delightful place, it wasn't lush or splashy or really upstage [posh] but it was really a nice, friendly, homely, healthy place to have. I stayed in it when I came up from a health break from Lindi. It was unfortunate that when the Mau-Mau troubles were at their height (their target was anything colonial) they burnt the Norfolk down. I thought this was a great tragedy because it would have been a historic monument for the city.

While in Nairobi, I somehow got into playing soccer for the Caledonians. How I met Caledonians I have no idea. As we started, playing in my first match for them, I remember thinking, well this is a pretty poor team, they've got no speed, nothing at all, but after the first ten to fifteen minutes I realised that playing football at 5,000 feet above sea level is a little different from playing it down on the fields of Kent!

But I enjoyed myself there very much, virtue of being young, just over 21 and very fit and healthy and looking forward to life in general. And I found life in general and in particular there; not only with the lads and lasses but also the older people, who introduce you to living in that type of place and living in the country. I learnt a great deal from talking about things that developed and would develop, and how problems happen and how to overcome problems.

Chapter 6:
Station Superintendent

Now Geoffrey really is on his own. He finds he has to do many things he's never done before - including driving a truck on some very interesting tracks - and manage a variety of problems, or can I just call them passengers?

It was in early '37 that John Blanco, the Area Manager, told me that he wanted me to take over Mbeya from Peter Edwards. As Peter had to travel rapidly, I was to meet him at Nairobi airport and discuss the takeover with him, and officially takeover the station at Nairobi airport, although I'd never even seen Mbeya. We spent a long session talking about the station, and the finances etc. It came as quite a surprise for me that I was in charge of everything at the station; although we had a station engineer there he was responsible only for the engineering on the aircraft. Anything else was the responsibility of me, the station superintendent.

Nairobi – Moshi – Serengeti

From Nairobi we took off in the Atalanta that was our Armstrong-Whitworth built aircraft I think it was AW15. It was a high wing monoplane 4-engine. At that time, we used a variety of aircraft going down from London to Johannesburg. We started off with the HP42, the European version, which was the Hannibal, between London and Paris; then there was the train down to Brindisi; then the flying boat which in those days was the Satyrus, the four-engined biplane, down to Alexandria. Then from Alexandria on down to Kisumu was the HP42 Tropical version, which was called the Heracles, and at Kisumu changed to the Atalanta, which was supposed to be our special aircraft built for high atmosphere and high landing operation because all the airports down past Kisumu were at least 5,500 ft high, some were even more.

The first section of the flight down as far as Moshi was incredibly interesting because it's over the Serengeti Plains, which while in those days they were absolute bush with one track through them, now of course they are the famous National Park which everybody pays enormous amounts of money to go and see. We used to see them just by taking a very careful trip out into the bush. But flying over them, you see a greater expanse of them, and you see more of them too. The skipper was always careful to fly at a reasonable height over them because as he said:

"It's wild animals, we don't want to start shooting them up and panicking them. The poor devils don't live long, they get scared out of their life. If we just go over them at normal altitude say 3,500 feet, we can see them well, we don't bother them too much, so they're happy and we're happy."

So that was the atmosphere.

Towards Moshi you see the wonderful views of Mt Kilimanjaro, in Tanganyika. It's a wonderful mountain, always snow-capped, ex-volcano and the centrepiece for hundreds of miles as a landmark. The one north of that is Mt Kenya, which also has snow on it all the year round but this is a totally different shape.

Mbeya

We eventually landed into Mbeya, which on approaching from the air is just like so many other places, a grassy area with a number of white stones around which indicate the area that has been 'cleared' and at least made sound so you won't normally sink into the surface. Outside the white markers which delineate the landing ground the grass would obviously be longer and you may find you got boggy ground around one side or the other.

We landed and I got out of the plane, I was met by the station clerk who was an Indian, as so many were in that position at that time. I never knew his name other than Singh. Then I realised the responsibilities I had that I'd never had before, of being the station manager, although then we were called Station Superintendent.

The first thing I had to do was allocate the rooms to the other passengers and crew! Well, I'd never seen the place before, but ably assisted by Singh, I allocated them and got him to mark up the baggage with room numbers, so the baggage could be taken up to the various rooms.

Next we checked with the skipper and the engineer about going on the next day, and arranged for weather reports from the stations south to be sent up so we'd get them in time. That was done by radio and came into Mbeya where there was a Government station, a telegraph station really, but this sort of radio was used for our navigational purposes because we had nothing else. The weather report used to come into the Post Office, because that ran the radio station in Mbeya, then a messenger would come out to us in the morning with it all typed up, telling us what the weather forecast was down the routes.

Having got that sorted out, I then asked the station clerk what happened to the mail.

"Well, sir, you take it in to Mbeya."

"Wait a minute; *I* have to take it in to Mbeya?"

"Yes, sir."

"Don't the Post Office collect it?"

"Oh, no, no, you take it in and deliver it to the Post Office in the town."

So I said, "How do I do that?"

He pointed to a half hundredweight Jowett van and said: "You get over there in that."

This shattered me. I'd never driven a car in my life, it was the first time I'd ever thought about it! So I made up my mind that I would in fact drive this vehicle, and I learnt, in jumps and jerks. Slowly I was able to get it off the airfield and onto the gravel track and get it into town, which was only about eight miles away, so I'd got plenty of time in order to be able to get there. With no other traffic it wasn't as if I'd have any complicated road control and road system, so I started jerking on my way, wondering if I was going to stall it, if I was going to kill the engine, or what I was going to do. I jerked along fairly well until I got to the top of one rise, and looking down to the other, I saw that there was a bridge over a stream! It was about four yards wide, but the bridge was nothing more than two rather thick logs, so laid that normally one could get one's wheels on, and get across. Well, I'd never seen this before and being scared stiff in the van, I didn't know what I would get up to. In the end, I made it but it was rather a case of trial and error, and hoping to God that I wouldn't get my wheels off the planks and finish either completely in the drink or half and half with the body being supported by these great big thick beams.

The number of times I got out and looked to see if I was still in line with these planks! I'd go back again and not run the engine and coast down the slope and get out again seeing that I was still in line. Even when I was just about on the beginning of the planks, I again got out and looked to see whether the car seemed lined up on the two. Then I started the engine and slowly, slowly eased myself and was I grateful when I found I was across! The only trouble was, of course, however much I was satisfied, I had to cross over again after delivering the mail – and by that time of course it would be dark! Anyway, I lived to tell the tale and that was my first lesson in driving.

Snakes alive!

The airport, well call it an airport, it was actually an airfield, of course, we just had an office and a brick store for the engineering spares, and then separately we had what we knew as 'the resthouse'.

This was fundamentally a hotel. It was built in a square, with the veranda around on the inside and a hole in the middle so that you had bags of air, mosquito proofed throughout of course. The front part of it was reception and lounges, then down either side you had the bedrooms, and across the back, the washrooms and toilets and the dining room, then on the other side you had the kitchen. Generally, the kitchens were outside the main block. There was no running water, so all the rooms had jugs of water and basins. If you wanted to have a bath, you had to order it a day in advance, so you could get the boys to boil up the water and pour enough for a bath, then come and tell you it was ready. Then you had to dash along for it before someone else found out and pinched your bath! The toilets were the old thunderboxes with buckets underneath and trapdoors at the back. The buckets were emptied overnight, which didn't really hurt anyone because most of the visitors were seasoned travellers and they understood that in places like Mbeya, right out in the bush, with no running water and anything like that, this was a sound and well accepted scheme of coping with the toilet requirement.

Early one evening, a woman passenger came rushing up saying "I've been bitten by a snake, bitten by a snake!"

I said, "what do you mean, bitten by a snake?"

"I've been bitten by a snake!"

I said: "You'd better go along to your room and I'll bring the snake kit along," because part of the first aid kit included a snake kit, with printed instructions. I don't know how you're supposed to read them before you started tackling the problem. Fortunately, I had a reasonable idea of what was required.

Having told the woman to go along to her room, and remembered which number it was, I remembered there was another woman passenger, the wife of a planter in Northern Rhodesia. I found her in the lounge and explained a snake had bitten this woman and asked her to help me fix it up.

She said, "oh, that's all right, leave it to me," so I gave her the so-called kit for snake bites and she went off to see this other woman. I was worried, because if a passenger were made ill on my station like that I'd be in real trouble. Care of the passengers was paramount and if you did something or omitted something so that any of the passengers were hurt or damaged it was as good as the sack!

After I'd been biting my nails for quite a while, the planter's wife came back grinning all over her face.

"What's going on, is she all right?" I said.

"Ah, don't worry, don't worry."

"Why not?"

"Well it wasn't a snake bite, it's quite all right."

"Well, what's going on?"

"She went along to the toilet, and when she was sitting on the thunderbox, something bit her bottom! She was scared stiff, thought it was a snake and reacted a bit. But I've just been along to look at this toilet and it's all right, there was a chicken in there, obviously went in there when they were changing the buckets during the night. It pecked her bottom and gave her such a fright! But she's all right now, she's had a gin so she'll be all right."

Balancing the books

The accounting at the station was the responsibility of the Station Superintendent. He was responsible for all the cash and all the expenditure, and all he could do was charge so much per night for what he provided, according to the book laid down by Head Office.

It was so much for passengers' dinner, overnight accommodation, breakfast, supplies put on the aircraft for the journey to the next station. You had to balance up your bar costs as well. Starting off without someone to hand it over in detail, it was a bit complicated trying to get track of it, but eventually we got it and I sort of got myself into a routine.

One day I found I just couldn't get the bar takings to balance and I had a long session with the boy that did the bar. He was perfectly reliable but I couldn't work out what was going on. We were talking about things and I found that there was a new tot (spirit measure) that had been sent down by the catering manager indicating there were so many tots in this bottle, so many in a bottle of whisky, or gin, and that we were to use that new measure from a certain date. The boy had obviously done that and started using this new tot according to the date as he was supposed to. But when we couldn't balance the books, and I thought he was dealing honestly, I thought, well, let's try this tot, and I found that in measuring a bottle of whisky using that tot there were fewer tots to the bottle than there were supposed to be. Every bottle was charged at a certain price, and the tots at a certain price, but it was a couple of tots short, so with each bottle of whisky or gin that was used I would have to pay for it (because I would have to square it up out of my own pocket).

So we went back to using the old measure and I wrote a stiff letter to the catering manager: how do you expect me to run my station if you fiddle us like that!

Most of the catering supplies that we used for meals were obtained from Mbeya. I thought to myself one day, collecting meat from there seems rather silly as I'm getting the grass cut here and we often turn up a buck. So next morning after our dawn departure, when the boys went out to do a spot more grass cutting, I went out with them and took the station rifle.

The way we did grass cutting, I think there were about ten local boys, and they had homemade implements like scythes. They each held a piece of thin flat iron of the sort one uses if one's making barrels. You bent the bottom nine or ten inches at right angles and sharpened both sides of it, you put a bit of rag round the other end, and the lads went off side by side swinging these things and that's it, that's how you mowed the grass and a jolly good job they did too. Out on the edges, where the grass had grown long, we didn't worry about it because it was outside the white markers, but frequently, with the boys laughing and shouting and giggling to themselves, we put up bush buck.

Going along with them on that morning, I saw a buck go up and it looked a reasonable size and a reasonably youngish one, so I shot it, and then the kitchen boy came out and we loaded it on to the little truck and took it back to the cook, who was delighted. He butchered it and, for three or four days, we had venison on the menu. We didn't have a written menu of course, it just came up, and there were comments after the meal, that it was rather nice meat, what was it? I said it was fresh venison obtained the previous morning. But the great advantage was that I was able to provide meat for the passengers without having to pay any money. It got favourable comment from the passengers and crew, who came though at reasonable intervals and knew what sort of meal they could expect at Mbeya. And later on when I had to balance the books I found that as a result of that I didn't have to charge myself or the station engineer any money for 'messing' because I'd been able to reduce the costs by not having to buy this meat. So everyone was very happy. We lived for nothing, I got my fun, the cook got his fun with the chopping up and so on he had to do, and he probably got rid of certain parts (the offal and so on) for his family or friends, and he wasn't cheating the company, either, so he was very happy.

I refer to the 'boys' frequently when I'm referring to the staff other than the European staff. Now I'm afraid I refer to the 'boys' like that in the 'colonial' way – it meant any of the local employees.

We did employ as many as the local employees as we could, as it was ridiculous to try to get some of the Europeans to do some of the jobs. Besides which we liked to live with the country as much as we could and we had the native, the local tribes, to do the jobs that had to be done. I did learn that there was one tribe that you had to be very careful of, and I've forgotten the name of it now, but you had to avoid ever taking them on as a houseboy because they did not believe in killing anything at all, no animals, no bugs, no fleas, anything. That was not really what you needed in a clean house!

Night stop routine

We had night stops a minimum of four times a week. The routine was quickly established as to what I had to do as the humble Station Super. The importance about the care of the passenger was deeply instilled into us as trainees, in fact into all the staff.

It started in the morning with the examination of the bedrooms: that they were clean, dusted, mosquito nets dusted, soap in dishes, and washbasins clean. There wouldn't be any water till nearer the arrival of the passengers, but I had to do a full inspection of the place including lounges, dining room, wash rooms, toilets and what bathrooms there were.

Of course, it was quite fun getting a signal from the station before they arrived telling us how many passengers there were and the breakdown, married or single, male or female. Obviously, you put married couples together and if you had enough vacant rooms you put all the others in singles. But if you were double night stopped (two planes in) then you got very tight and you had to double up the males with other males and the females with other females. Fortunately, there wasn't a high number of females travelling so it didn't make it too complicated, but there was always the odd occasion when the rooms would be allocated and afterwards a fellow would come along asking if he could be put in a room next door to Miss so-and-so. There was always a certain amount of endeavouring by certain male passengers and occasionally a female passenger to see if they could share a room at a resthouse.

The most embarrassing time I had was one morning when the boy went around and made the usual early morning calls: he came back to me and said he didn't get any reply from number five room.

I looked up the passenger list and saw that number five was a Mrs so-and-so. I went and knocked on the door, no answer, knocked on the door again, no answer, rattled the door, no answer, and in the end I went in, and there I found a lady, flat out, absolutely starkers [naked], lying almost cruciform on her back on the bed. Clothes lay all round the room and she really was flat out. I realised that she had been drinking rather heavily during the evening and had obviously gone to bed very tight and didn't know quite what was happening to her. But trying to wake her up, of course, was an urgent thing, because we had to get her away with the other passengers, and otherwise she was in trouble. Well, I would be anyway, because she would miss the plane and that would be my fault.

If she did miss the plane, it meant that she'd have to wait for two or three days before the next one came through, and there might not be room on it in which case she'd have to wait another two or three days. In any case she would be forfeiting that section of her fare and she would have to pay that extra one another time. So with cold flannels and water in the jug, I slapped her around with cold water and shook her, but got very little response and I thought, well what do I do now? I daren't go along and see if there was another woman passenger and get her to look after her because that just creates a nonsense further on during the trip. So I carefully dragged the woman around and worked out what clothes there were around. At that time, I didn't have any idea what a woman wore under her dress and certainly didn't know how to put these things on! It was new territory for me. So somehow I got her decently covered and in such a position to stand up as long as I gave her a lot of support.

I packed the rest of what I could find in her room into her suitcase, left her sitting in the chair there, and went down to see how the plane was doing.

The engineer said it was alright and would be leaving on time, "you can start loading the passengers in about ten minutes."

"Well, I'll bring in an early one."

"What do you mean?" he asked.

I explained we'd got one very drunk still, a real bangover [sic] and I wanted to get her on the plane before the others, so it didn't become too obvious. He told me which seat to put her in so she wouldn't seem obvious, and back I went to the resthouse.

I went up to her room, lifted her up and dragged her out of the resthouse and down the steps. I manhandled her across the grass, and up into the aircraft, and put her down in the seat that the engineer had recommended, and put a blanket round her and strapped her in. Then I kept my fingers crossed and hoped for the best!

Back in the resthouse I looked after the other passengers, and mentioned to them that one of the other passengers wasn't feeling too well and she'd already been loaded, but she was sitting quietly in the back and not to worry too much about her, and they appeared to accept this explanation.

I never heard any more about it so I can only presume that everything was all right. Quite honestly the position of walking in on this naked lady sprawled over the bed and somehow getting her into a condition to get her into the aeroplane somewhat taxed my ingenuity but, well, we made it.

I'd never run a hotel before but there I was running the resthouse, so we all learn. The whole idea was you had to learn and learn quickly.

Chapter 7:
Lindi

At Mbeya, Imperial Airways were still using land planes for the link down to the Cape. The most exciting development was about to take place, the extension of the flying boat service all the way down through Africa. This meant water – rivers, lakes or the sea – for the flying boats to land, of course. I once described Geoffrey to friends as an aviation pioneer. Mostly we think of the flyers as the real pioneers, but this phase of Geoffrey's life was probably the one he enjoyed most – he really was pioneering the ground services for the flying boat service in the stations he was posted to. As we will see, that meant creating something from scratch most of the time, and not always with the support of the local British officials. He always spoke of Lindi with love in his voice. To me it is a place of magic.

In May 1937 I went back up to Nairobi and was put on planning for the extension of the C Class flying boats down the route to South Africa. Well, not planning the routing of course but places en route: we had to have stations, and those had to be equipped and some of the proposed stations could be just bare places with no facilities. So it was necessary to have a plan that if one of these places was appointed as a landing stage then we would quickly be able to do what was necessary in order to make it habitable and possible for a duty number of staff and boats to go through.

So I was told to draw up a plan on the basis that the 'boat was going to land at a place where there was nothing. This included the launches and marine equipment, the boys and the night landing equipment and that sort of thing, but also the places for living. One could presume there was some sort of building there to get into, even if it was only a mud hut put up by the local native boys, but you'd also got to have beds, bed linen, mosquito nets, pots, pans, paraffin lights, paraffin stove, paraffin supplies, canned food (so that if you were really in trouble you could exist until you'd established yourself), everything to make life possible. We did assume that there would be a water supply available. It was the only thing that we were charged to forget about in planning a station. So I got down to doing this business on paper, and I found it was quite fun, actually, all the little things one would consider necessary in life!

There were several places where this might have been required and I seem to remember now that there was Butiaba, Laropi, Naivasha and Lindi. Bill Linstead visited to Laropi; he went up to do a last minute survey of it, whether or not it was a practical place for landing. He found it pretty rough up there, but I always remember the chart he drew of the area which included places like Tusker Point and Walker Lagoon, and Booth Stretch, every place was named after some kind of drink that was known about the area at that time! I was told quite suddenly to go down to Lindi; I didn't know where it was, on the coast of East Africa, down by the Portuguese border, that was it, that was where it was shown on the map. I knew nothing about it, and it was fortunate that I had already done planning for such an eventuality and I pulled out the plans for one station and went through them rapidly to see if I'd left anything out!

Introduction to Lindi

In fact things worked out rather well. I was flown down to Lindi on a Leopard Moth, I seem to remember by Captain Mostyn who was the chief pilot of what was then Wilson Airways (which was a charter company in those days). He flew me down in the Leopard from Nairobi to Mombasa then from Mombasa to Dar Es Salaam where I met a buddy of mine who had been a trainee two years before me, and then I met him again when he was with BEA and he was manager in Turkey. We stayed the night in Dar Es Salaam and the following day, 26th May 1937, we went off down to Lindi. We did an interim stop at Tanga, which was nothing more than a very small grass strip. One end went off into the bush and the other went over a cliff down into the water. You'd want a pretty skilful pilot to get in and get out.

We went on down to Lindi and found there was virtually no aerodrome. Well, there was one, but it was miles out of town and it was grass overgrown and we couldn't land on it. So Mostyn did a circle around the village, well, there were one or two buildings on what looked like a quay with a very small jetty. He looked around and he said, "right we'll land there," and aimed for the sandy beach on the north side of town.

We landed all right and he pulled up, and just after we pulled up and I'd got out, a little truck came up and we found it was the Shell man, who asked if we wanted any fuel. Mostyn said, "yes, thank you very much, "and they got on with refuelling the plane.

I got my bags out and looked around and thought, yes, now what do I do? And I realised from now on I was on my own. Nobody there had been advance notified that I was coming, I was just there with my suitcase and that was it.

The previous evening in Dar Es Salaam, Mostyn had been keen to get in touch with the Met people, particularly to find out what the position of tides was. Having landed on the beach I realised that he didn't want to get down when the tide was high as then he'd be in the really soft sand and he'd never be able to make it. So I had got one lesson learnt just as I landed there. When he was refuelled Mostyn turned his aircraft round, waved me goodbye and said "I'll see you sometime, I suppose," and off he went.

The Shell representative asked me where I was going to stay.

"I don't know, is there a hotel?" I asked.

"Hotel! We haven't got such a thing like that here!"

"Oh. I don't know what I'm going to do - and I'd better check in with the immigration officer because I've just come down from Kenya into Tanganyika and I ought to report."

He said, "well that's all right, that's the Chief of Police. I can take you up there as I've got my little office just up around that area."

So I piled onto the truck, which also carried the petrol, and went off to see the policeman.

The Officer in Charge was a superintendent and he was, I gather, the Superintendent of the whole of the Lindi official area. In his way he was an important person. He had a number of native police under him and he had the prison, too, as I found when I went to his house, which was a wing of the prison compound. I reported in to him as an immigrant from Kenya, he looked at my passport and noted what he needed and we settled down to chat. He asked me where I was going to stay and I said I hadn't a clue. It turned out he was on his own as his wife was on leave, and I could quite easily use his spare room until we found out what was going on, so that's what happened.

The rest of the stuff I needed was due on the steamer, the *Bardia*, which was a monthly steamer. This wasn't due in till about three days later, so I was very grateful to have the accommodation, and have somewhere to rest myself until such time as we got all the stuff that was supposed to come on the boat. That was one of the problems for me, to sit there and wait and wonder if the planning I'd done in Nairobi would be satisfactory, as if it wasn't it would be my own fault. After all I'd planned for the equipping of a house, an office, the flying boat, the launches, the radio pack set, all these sort of things, now it was time to sit down and keep my fingers crossed. I hoped what I'd done in the office up in Nairobi was satisfactory and would prove I had done a decent job, as I was the one that was going to suffer if I hadn't!

Thanks to the local Public Works Department officer, I was able to find an empty bungalow along the beach about half a mile from town. I say town but it was just a few dookas and three or four shacks and a jetty and warehouses. During this time I was able to call on the District Commissioner who was the boss of the area, and was introduced to the Marine Superintendent who in charge of the maritime side, the port and everything that went on in the port. So I was able to establish things before the equipment arrived.

I'd met the Customs Officer, of course, because I saw him when I arrived on the plane. The other official, Fred Hersey, became quite a pal of mine over the time I was there. He was the Port Health Authority and as such he was an important person from a business point of view for my passengers and the aircraft travelling out of East Africa and into Portuguese East, as Portuguese East [Africa] at that time had some quarantine restrictions.

The senior government officer was the District Commiss-ioner, he was responsible for the whole of the Lindi District politically and administratively. There was the District Officer who, apart from touring around and seeing that things were all right and justice was done, was also the chief magistrate of the area; there was the assistant District Officer, the Medical Officer who ran the hospital there along with his wife and there was a nursing sister there who was the equivalent of the matron of a hospital.

The roads and so on were looked after by the Public Works Department officer and there was also an agriculture officer and the ports officer. The Ports Officer was (as usual) a Scotsman; I forget what his name was but where in the world at that time did you find a port superintendent that was not a Scotsman?

There was the bank manager and an assistant bank manager – the bank was Barclays DCNO, which was almost universal in British East Africa. Apart from the Bank Manager and his assistant, all the rest were government officials. The only other people would become me and my coxswain who would make up the total of four non-government officials in the white population of the area.

In the village there were about ten Indian families. I don't know exactly how many because I'm afraid I didn't make any contact with them, apart from the Customs Officer and the fellow that managed the local shop. I call it a shop; he traded in just about everything that the native population might like to buy.

Sisal estates

Outside Lindi I remember two particular sisal estates, which were owned, well I don't know whether they were owned, but they were managed by whites. There was one out at Kikwetu, which was up north from us about 10-15 miles north from Lindi. Two lads from there used to come up occasionally to Lindi to meet somebody else and have a chat and they were very good; they had a guitar and they used to settle down and we'd have wonderful sing-songs with them.

The other estate was run by Pop Gage, he seemed to be ancient, but he couldn't have been that old - he was very fit. He was short, very thick, quite stout, not stout but thick-set. He was a bundle of energy. His estate was a bit nearer, it was a wonderful one called Mbangawanga.

The great feature about it was, in order to be able to get around his estate without having to make roads or tracks, he salvaged the sleeper and rails from the railway built by the Germans when they had occupied that part of East Africa. With these he built a circuit around his estate (I don't know how many acres it was but the circuit was certainly many miles). He built this and laid the track and then he got some flanged wheels so he could then make a carriage, and more flanged wheels so he could make an engine. And on that platform he built a car engine which, I don't know how, communicated its action onto the rear wheels and so made himself a motor-car-train that used to go around his estate. He also used it for carting the bales of sisal from one place to another. It solved an enormous amount of problems in transporting his particular product.

The product of course was sisal, and they were particularly known for their sheds where they had their decordicators. A decordicator was a place where they mashed the leaves and got all the juices and dressing out of it and finished up with only the fibres left, which when dried made your sisal. But the decordicator had the most foul stench – it really was a most revolting scent, but you know it came out of the sisal, it was a natural aroma, and nothing anybody could do except say "well, that's nature in the raw."

Pop Gage was a wonderful character; he occasionally asked people out for the weekend to stay at his place and they were memorable. The thing I remember about it most was that we had beds out on the verandas, of course with mosquito net. But he was in his room, which generally was across the other side of the bungalow, and he had the most marvellous snore and it really roared around his bungalow. It used to really amuse us visitors, and we used to really enjoy our weekend, not just the relaxation because he was a jolly good host, but this snoring really was a highlight of the weekend!

Setting up Lindi Station

With the arrival two or three days later of the *Bardia* – the ship that had got all our equipment - on its routine monthly visit, also came Bob Percival who was the coxswain who had been posted to the station.

Fortunately, Bob Percival was an East African, he wasn't born there but he had been there many years, and he did speak fairly fluent Swahili, so that we had no problem then in recruiting native staff.

Having found a bungalow about half a mile to the north of the village up the coast, almost on the shore, we then arranged for our stores to be moved into that house and we tried to settle in and make ourselves at home. Bob Percival was able to recruit a cook and the staff necessary to run the house and I found accommodation that we could use as an office and as an engine spares store. So we were almost getting down to work apart from the provision for the boats.

For the two big launches, we had to find an anchorage, in fact we had to lay our own anchorage. There was nothing there to moor them to but we got them on the water and anchored. The next job was to survey the alighting area to check that it was clear of problems and to mark up and buoy those obstructions in the area of the estuary that might become hazardous to flying boats manoeuvring. And, a big problem of course, to lay the moorings.

Charts and moorings

I spent quite a while in the small launch going to and fro across the estuary, poling my way across, dipping the pole down to check the depths. I was only interested in depths in excess of ten feet because fortunately I was able to do this below the area of Low Water Springs. If there was ten feet of water at Low Water Springs (LWS) then there was a helluva lot of water when tides were normal. But this did give me the opportunity of checking the extent of a big sandbank in the river mouth, which had a wonderful name - it was called Fungal Mbati Wanaki. I love that name; it's beautiful isn't it. Because it was shallow at LWS I decided it was necessary to mark up as a possible obstruction and arrange to have the edges of it buoyed. Subsequently in the maps that I drew of the area for our aircrew I was able to mark out the area of danger, where the currents were and where there was obviously very clear water. It was also necessary to mark the area of navigation for the 'official' boats that came into and out of the river. Not that there were many that came, there was only really the *SS Bardia* and she came once a month anyway. There were a few dhows that came up the estuary, but they were not of much importance to the operation.

From my point of view, I had to get a chart of the flying boat area, landing area, and mooring areas, drawn out so that they could be reproduced and circulated among the aircrews. It was interesting that on one run across the estuary I suddenly hit a rock which came in a normal low water run, and it was obvious that at LWS it would be just at the sea surface, so technically it was an obstruction not just for the flying boats but also for the steamers. I examined the maritime chart of the area, but it didn't show the rock despite it being in the area marked for safe anchorage for ships. So I made my name reporting this to the Maritime Board and it was then incorporated in the East African Pilot as a third class amendment to the charts.

We didn't really have any problem in laying the aircraft moorings, although when showing the plans to the superintendent he asked what we were supposed to be mooring. When I said this was the official plan for a two mooring stage for the flying boats he said, "what are they because those moorings would hold the Queen Mary here!" But while he laughed, he realised that instructions from Head Office are such that you carry them out, and I was able, through him, to get a contractor to lay the moorings instead of having to do them myself, which would have been a very tricky job without any facilities. But the local Indian contractor was able to do it with his own equipment, barges and tugs and things like that. We paid him for doing the job and insured him against any danger to his staff. Fortunately, they laid the moorings where we wanted them and without damage to any of the natives that he used as labour.

Communications

Communication between Lindi and the outside world was very scant. The mail only came in on the *Bardia*, which was as I said a monthly routine visit; she came down from Mombasa and Dar Es Salaam. Otherwise, there was the single wire telegraph wire between Lindi and Dar Es Salaam. This was very unreliable because (a) it depended on an earth-return circuit and (b) the wire was strung on posts that made wonderful places for elephants to scratch their backs against. Time and time again the posts were down and the post and telegraphs people had to go out and work out where the posts had been broken and go out and repair the circuits. It was a hazardous thing but that was the only communication. So the people in Lindi were looking forward with considerable anticipation to connecting to the world by a flying boat service.

I don't remember having any communication with my headquarters in Nairobi, other than one letter (by surface mail) that said they didn't want to hear from me until I reported that the station would be fully operational as from the 1st July 1937. I don't remember what time this was before that particular date - although my arrival at Lindi was the 26th May - all I remember was that Bob Percival and I kept doing what we needed to do in order to create a viable flying boat transit station by that deadline.

I sent a telegram via Dar Es Salaam saying I considered the station was operational well in time for 1st July, then I sat down and waited for an indication that the services would start. Any communication that I got was usually from my headquarters in Nairobi down to Pat Haywood who was the station superintendent at Dar Es Salaam and then he would pass on a message by the landline telegraph down to me, provided the landline was available. It was useless to use any other system.

Lindi is operational

There was great excitement on the day we had our first flying boat land. It was coming southbound from Dar Es Salaam and everything went according to the plan that we had always thought of. Except, of course, that the locals were most intrigued to see the flying boat land and to see what went on.

Everything to them was so new and so amazing because they'd only ever been used to the once a month coastal steamer coming through or there might have been some trading dhows coming down from the Red Sea but that was all! To have this flying boat coming in and landing, the magnificent flying machine coming down and landing on the water, beautiful spray coming up till she'd settled down, and then taxiing to the moorings, which were satisfactory, which were picked up well and truly by the radio operator; the launches operated well and truly, and, you know, the customs officer came on board with us on the auxiliary launch, and the port health officer came on board in order to inspect health documents, and everyone was exceedingly happy!

That was the start of the regular operation, and from Geoffrey's photographs it may have been Calpurnia that made that first landing. With two flights going in each direction each week, there were soon plenty of incidents to report, although also periods of great boredom. They had to make their own entertainment.

The Radio Tree

We were in the little offices we got originally, we got our radio pack set up and got our aerial up on the coconut tree across the track outside, and we were able to work the aircraft all right and that was fine. But one day the police superintendant came along to me and asked how it was going, and general pleasantries, and then: "I'm afraid I've got trouble for you."

"Trouble?" I said.

"Yes, apparently the tree that you've got your aerial attached to, the fellow that owns it is complaining that you're killing the spirit of the tree."

It was the screeching and the horrible noises as I tortured the tree before I killed it. So he was trying to get the police superintendant to get me to abandon my work against his tree or alternatively I would have to compensate him for killing his tree.

I explained to the police superintendant that obviously the noises were the atmospherics that he'd heard. The dits and dots and dashes that the operator was sending out were obviously in our office and nothing at all to do with the tree, but somehow we'd got to pacify this fellow. I thought that maybe we could do it by showing him how clever his tree was and with our wire attached to it, the tree could talk to the aeroplane. The aeroplane to them was a bird flying in the sky and something great, so I thought this might work. With the police super's help, we got the owner of this tree (he wasn't a very important local chief or anything like that, he was just a tribal member of the area) and he told him that he would be able to witness this.

On the day there was a boat coming in, we got our radio operator to get in touch with the plane's radio operator to ask them if they would shoot off a couple of Very lights as they flew over the landing area just before they circled and landed. I said to tell the skipper that it would help me solve political problems on the ground if he could do it. We got a message back very soon saying 'ok, one red and one white'. So we then said to the owner of the tree that his tree had taken our message to the aeroplane and we would have to see what the aeroplane did in way of an answer – we didn't tell him exactly what we had asked for. We waited until the plane flew over the alighting area and sure enough, as she flew, out came one Very light and then another Very light. This was terrific, he was absolutely thrilled with it.

After landing, I explained to the skipper why I'd asked him to do this, and he thought it was a jolly good idea.

"Have you solved the problem," he said.

"I don't know yet, I've got to wait till I get back."

So, after he left I had a word with the police superintendant.

"Are we still in trouble?"

"No, no, no," he replied. "He thinks that's lovely, he knows his tree can talk to the aeroplane, it's absolutely marvellous. But I should be careful because any minute now he'll come back to you and say 'since it's my tree talking to the aeroplane can I send a message to the aeroplane,' so watch out for a further approach!"

Boy trouble

The moorings we had laid early on were great big red rubber buoys that floated on the surface, They held the main line that went down to the sinker – the riser chain - and attached to the riser chain was a rope with a loop on it. That rope was propped up on top of the mooring buoy so that, as the skipper approached the buoy, the radio operator could lean out and grab it and put it over the bollard, which was a retractable one on the nose of the flying boat.

When we were in regular operations, we would make regular checks of our alighting area and the moorings and so on. On one occasion, we found the riser chain was tangled around the main chain and the mooring line, therefore would have been fouled. So I asked one of the boys to dive down and untangle it from the chain. They jibbed a bit at this and said they were local boys and didn't go diving in the water. So I thought, well, it's not worthwhile arguing about it, let's get on and do it. So I just stripped off and dived over and took myself down the chain until I felt where the rope was tangled, and came up and had a few breaths and went down again and untangled the chain and the rope and let it float away. Then I came up and we picked it up on a boathook and put it on top of the buoy.

Now to me, having mucked about in the sea at Tankerton when I was a kid and mucking about in the sea at Rochester and Brindisi with the flying boats, it didn't strike me as anything extraordinary, but it was interesting that after that, if anything needed to be done on or in the water, I had no trouble at all with any of the native crew diving in and doing their work underneath. It was the example I'd given them. I found subsequently that any of these native boys, if they knew you could do it yourself then they would get on and do it. If on the other hand you said you wanted something done and they said they couldn't do it and you couldn't do it yourself, then they got one over you and from then on it was very difficult to control your manpower.

We were getting a terminal building built on the edge of the river, and I wanted the area in front of the terminal area made look reasonably respectable. I'd had a whole load of the coral rocks that lay around and bleached white in the sun brought in, and I wanted the boys to put them around to make a perimeter track. In this way you had the area in front of the building with a white outline to the land that we claimed, more or less as our own. But I had great problems there, they couldn't do that, and I indicated they just had to get on and do it.

They said no, no, they were boat boys they weren't labourers.

I said well if you won't get on and do it you're all sacked!

And they were delighted for that, because they knew that afternoon there was going to be a flying boat through, so they thought they were really on a good wicket.

But later on when the flying boat arrived, the coxswain and I coped with the flying boat on our own using only the small launch and everything worked almost as though the boys had been working with us. And once again, later on, no trouble at all!

They came back and they said yes, they would do the stone movement around, and consequently I took them back on as members of my staff again, and I never had any more trouble at all.

Social Life with a sting in the tail

With only about ten or twelve families there in Lindi you can imagine that entertainment there was very limited, in fact it was a case of entertaining each other more or less round the clock, but at different houses. We did however have a clubhouse which was built. It was a nice clubhouse really with a bar and a veranda with some tables outside on the veranda in the shade. It was on the beach, overlooking the sea; it was very pleasant. At the same time, there was a concrete tennis court built behind it, on the other side of the coastal road, and there I really learned to play tennis. It was while I was at Nairobi I was sort of initiated into playing tennis, I'd bought myself a racquet to play with Stefani White and his wife and also Harold; he and his wife also lived in the same little hotel – he subsequently became a mayor of Nairobi.

So I had got used to having a racquet and a few balls to knock over a net and I knew the basic rules of playing tennis. As there was nothing else to do there and everyone else wanting to have parties or play games, I was always prepared to have a knock up with anyone who happened to come along. I was the rabbit of the lot; nobody thought or even hinted that I was a brilliant tennis player, but if I was prepared to bash the ball across to people and they were prepared to bash it back to me, okay, we entertained each other.

Other than that of course was the swimming. Naturally, one swam frequently because our bungalow was right on the shore. You just came out of the bungalow down the sand into the sea and, in normal circumstances, it was perfectly all right, no trouble at all.

But certain times of the year when there are stinging jellyfish and sting you they would. I remember one time I was swimming along and I saw the telltale blue float ahead of me, and I said, "uh-oh Portuguese Man-O-War", and turned round and swam away. Well, that was the worst thing to do because in turning round I wrapped the sting, which was already past me, I wrapped the sting around my waistline and it was very painful. I put everything on it I could possibly think of to stop the stinging but nothing seemed to stop it. Around my waistline, I got what looked like two rows of stitches, just as if I'd been put under a sewing machine and turned over and over and the sewing machine needle going up and down all the time all around my tummy. It was very painful indeed and I didn't know what to do about it, having tried everything I knew. I went up to see the local doctor and he apologised that he didn't know! Nobody seemed to know what to do to counteract the sting of the Portuguese Man-O-War. All he could recommend doing was to put some grease on it, whatever grease I had, and suffer it!

Apart from silly things like that it was really lovely swimming because the water was very clear and it was not often we had really rough weather because we were in the estuary of the river. It was clean because there was no pollution. The steamer came in only once a month and the only other ships that came in were the Arab sailing boats that came down from the Gulf; that was all that was done to it and it really was nice and clear and warm, sometimes in fact it was too warm! It was thoroughly enjoyable swimming.

The people at Lindi were a very happy crowd. They were very decent people and there was never any trouble or embarrassment and it really was one of the happiest stations that I've ever been at. Everybody knew that life was pretty rough and pretty tough in Lindi so everybody did what they could to keep themselves and other people reasonably happy.

Chicken dinners

In the food line, we produced no local fruit at all, there was nothing like that locally unless you could call coconuts fruit, and any fruit or fresh vegetables had to come in by steamer from Dar Es Salaam. I was very lucky: I arranged with Pat Haywood in Dar Es Salaam to send me down some vegetables and fruit on one flight a week, so Bob Percival and myself in the bungalow had some fresh fruit. People were delighted to be invited to have an evening meal with us, because they always knew they'd get some sort of vegetables that were reasonably fresh, and some fruit, which was stewed, but fresh compared with anything else that they might have.

Tinned meat was available through the Indian dooka, other things were available, but it was tinned, tinned, tinned, as there was very rarely anything fresh in the dooka.

Other than the tinned meat, there was chicken, which you had to breed yourself and the boy went and killed it and cleaned it and cooked it. That way you had devilled chicken for breakfast, boiled chicken for lunch, roast chicken for evening meal, and then a combination of any of those in curry or whatever you had. So that the bungalow, the two of us, we reckoned on our mess bill that we ate thirty chicken a month!

The only other fresh meat we got was from our share of the one sheep that was killed and passed round in the village, for everybody, the Indians as well as the British families. This was apportioned according to the number of people per household, which virtually meant that we got probably the equivalent of a quarter of a pound of fresh red meat once a month. I mean between the two of us, not each!

Other flights

Occasionally a land plane came in; a very small monoplane with a maximum of four people on it, including the pilot, would sometimes appear overhead without any advance information about them coming. Fortunately, they were all advised of the drill for landing at Lindi, which was to fly over the village and look at the beach. If it looked all right then they could land on it, if not they had to go off to the landing area; it was at least five miles to the landing area which was just a cleared area with not too tall grass on it.

After we'd established ourselves in the bay as *the* people in connection with aeroplanes, we occasionally used to go out to this area to see what it was like, to see that the jungle hadn't really taken it over again. Then we'd get the Public Works Department people to go and visit it to slash the grass down and to see that the white edging stones, that showed technically where the landing area was, were showing reasonably through the grass and showing up white.

But we also started a drill which we found worked: if the beach was all right we didn't take any notice, but if it wasn't all right, particularly if it started getting corrugated or waved or something like that, we'd go out on the sand and draw a big circle with a cross in it, indicating that the landing was unsafe. So that when they saw that sign, someone was warning them that something was wrong and so they didn't attempt to land on the beach.

If they did circle us and find that the landing wasn't all right, they'd go off to the airstrip and by the time we realised, they'd come and gone. We'd get in touch with the petrol bloke, so he could load up his van with some petrol because eventually he would have to take petrol out to the plane, since the only reason for landing is to refuel. So then we'd hurry out along the unmade roads to the airfield to find out how the fellow was, who he was, where he was going, if he was staying, if he wanted fuel, if he'd cleared Customs, if he'd got immigration problems, if the engine was ok, if the aeroplane was serviceable to carry on and if so where he was going, so that we could tell those where he was going that he was coming! It was a lot of fun, but it was the sort of thing that we at Imperial Airways did, because in those days we were the only people that had anything to do with anything in the air. There were virtually no RAF stations around and no other air force around and if there was an aeroplane around then it was expected that they could depend on the Imperial Airways bloke, whoever they were, wherever they were, to do their best to look after them.

Blind Landings

We had our own radio operator, he was Mark Ray, and the official Marconi man was posted to Lindi because they looked at it as a Communications Centre operated by the Marconi people. So they posted down to us their initial operator, that was Mike Murphy. That was absolutely marvellous, because he had previously been operator on aeroplanes operating for Rollason, I think, one of the small flying clubs that were operating at Croydon; he knew the drill of air transport. He was a nice fellow too and we had lots of time to swap stories, particularly about Croydon and what he'd done there and flying around various parts of Europe.

It happened we were sitting in the club, on the lounge having a little quiet beer, and we started discussing the possibility of blind weather landings. It then struck us that we, in Airways, had no instructions as to what to do if weather closed down, and there was no alternative for a pilot to be able to go to an alternative alighting area: the nearest one was about three hundred miles away!

After a long chat and poring over charts and things, we thought it might be a good idea to get the pilot to fly over the station, so we could get engines overhead and then to be able to direct him on a course which would safe for him to use as an alighting area. Then you have to work out the details of that - the problem being to get the pilot to fly over the top of the radio station in order to be able to get him in right positions. You've also got to pre-plan, so that once you've got him over the radio station you know the route to send him on that will keep him clear so that he can slowly lose height and, after a while, touch down on the sea without diving into it or crashing into one of the hills around. This is where Mike's experience came in, and we did work out what might be a good drill.

On the next flight coming in, we spoke to the skipper, and asked him if he would mind doing a test for us for a possible idea for bad weather landings, and he said he would. So Mike got doing his stuff and tried to get him over the top, and of course we could see him all right so it worked fairly well. Then we took him over the top of us and sent him on the course that we thought was a good safe one, and the rate of descent that we thought was safe, and asked him to do that. I was in the launch for this, out in the bay, and slowly the aircraft came in and touched down.

He followed me in, we tied up, moored the aircraft and had a word with the skipper.

"Yes," he said, "it works jolly well. Provided you get me over the top of you like you did at the height that you did, then the track is right and the loss of height's right and you're in the right position, then everything seems to work very well. So if everything else fails, it's worth a try."

So, that was what Mike and I put together and we kept up our sleeves hoping that one of these days, if anything went wrong, we'd got something to pull out of the hat.

On one occasion, the launch had cast off and we'd gone out onto the water to see everything was clear for landing. We got the message from Mike and the radio station what the landing time was, and from that time on we were cut off from the radio station, because we didn't have a radio in our launch. So we did our usual routine patrol, and just as we were starting, the weather closed down, it came down real torrential rain and great billowing clouds came through as well, and I said to myself, well, what are we going to do now? I hoped that Mike remembered what we'd talked about a month or so earlier, so we went out through the rain and the splash to where there was a big deep channel-marking buoy, which was there solely for helping the steamer coming in up the channel. We went out there because we thought that was the position to be if the aircraft came the way we planned. We switched off our engine so we could listen and hear if the aircraft went over.

Sure enough, we heard the aircraft way over in the distance in the direction of the radio station, so we kept our fingers crossed and it came nearer and nearer. Suddenly it emerged through the murk and I fired a Very pistol just so he could see it and know we'd seen him. He slowly eased his throttle back, touched down and splashed, and then we lost him in the rain!

We chased after him because we could see his wake, picked him up and got ahead of him, then led him back slowly to the mooring area and got him hitched up. By this time, we were absolutely drenched because the rain was still pouring down and visibility was very poor indeed. Anyway, we got aboard and stripped ourselves off, went up and said hello to the skipper, and he was delighted, he thought it was a wonderful scheme and he was full of congratulations to the radio operator and the station for the way we had handled guiding him into position. When I told him that fortunately we were lucky in this lad who had been flying at Croydon with Rollason, he realised that yes, we were very lucky indeed. It was subsequently reported to our Head Office and I gather that they made that as the standing bad weather drill for Lindi station.

M'beriali

What to call a flying boat in local Swahili was a bit of a problem.

They already knew a land plane and up country the land plane was called the *ndege*, which was Swahili for bird, well it was just a thing that flew through the air, it was a bird. But here was this thing that also came down on the water, what was this? It couldn't be *ndege* because although that flies through the air, it lands on the water like a ship, but it couldn't be a ship it was an aeroplane. So what we do – ah yes, it brings the mail in, doesn't it? Instead of the mail coming on the steamer once a month, it now comes in on the flying boat, so why not call it the *maili?* But the steamer is called the *maili* because the *maili* brings the mail in. And now the mail comes in on the flying boat. But you can't call it a *maili* because it isn't a steamer!

So there was a great argument among the local natives on how to describe the flying boat and in the end they gave up, and said, ah well, it's looked after by Imperial Airways, and they've got a word for Imperial Airways which was just *m'beriali*. So from then on, the flying boat was always referred to as *m'beriali* because that was the thing that was operated by Imperial Airways.

HMS Emerald

Mike Murphy rang me from his Marconi radio station to tell me that he had a peculiar call, on the air, for someone wanting to know what time the flying boat was arriving.

"Who is it that wants to know?" I asked.

"I don't know, because he was very chary about identification, and quite frankly I think it must be a navy ship, the keying is that sort of thing and the type of message is very controlled, I think it must be a naval ship of some sort."

I thought, well, there's no harm in giving the information, so I gave him the ETA.

A little while later Mike came back on the phone, and said, "yes, I've got a message; they're still not saying who they are but asking the question what time would it be necessary for the mail to arrive in Lindi in order to combine with the flying boat?"

And I thought, well, something's going on, but what? I estimated half an hour would do for swapping mail over and gave him the time.

"Righto, I'll let you know if anything happens."

A little while later I got the message: Stand by to receive a flying boat (at such and such a time) with mail for the north bound flying boat coming from HMS Emerald.

So we had fun then because we'd never had this sort of thing happen before!

Suddenly we saw a catapult-launched flying boat coming in. We did our usual drill of showing him where we wanted him to land and took him up to where we wanted him to buoy, because at that time our flying boat hadn't arrived and we wanted to put him on the mooring we wouldn't be putting the flying boat on. He came up, moored and passed us over some mail and we signed some papers for him. Just then the flying boat appeared. The visitor said he'd stay on the water until after it had landed, so we took his mail, landed our flying boat and the visitor went off. He mentioned just before leaving that he was from HMS Emerald and that Emerald would be coming in to Lindi port to pay a courtesy visit to the Governor in a couple of days' time. And I thought: oh, that's very interesting, thank you very much! He went off and we carried on with our flying boat. We added the fleet mail to our local mail, loaded up and sent off the flying boat.

The next day a message came over from Dar Es Salaam to the District Commissioner Lindi, indicating that Emerald would be coming in to Lindi on a given day and time and they were expected to carry out the 'normal courtesies'. This was fine, I didn't know what the 'normal courtesies' were, that was a political matter. We were just bystanders for that sort of thing. So we waited the arrival of the Emerald, she moored and the local governor was on the quayside by the jetty, and the naval pinnace came in with all flags flying, and approached the jetty. I indicated to the coxswain at the jetty not to come down to the side but to come to the end, because although there were steps on the side, I knew it was hazardous for launches because of my own experience in Lindi. So I indicated he come to the end, but oh no, he came around obviously as instructed by his officers and pulled up at the side of the jetty where the steps were, and the inevitable 'clonk, clonk!' Yes, he'd fouled his underwater gear!

They moored, and the Captain of the vessel landed, did his stuff with the District Commissioner and they went off. I spoke to the coxswain, the naval coxswain, and said "what's the trouble?"

He said, "oh we're really in trouble, we've broken the underwater gear or something and we're going to be in trouble now."

A little later on our District Commissioner requested me to make our big launch available to the navy for whatever needed to be done.

"I can only do that provided I have my own crew using it, I'm not having any other crews using it," I said.

In the end, the Captain of the Emerald agreed that I could use my crew, which was rather fun, as my crew had seen how the navy crew were doing their stuff when they were coming in, their drill and so on. We didn't have any drill like that, but the lads, the natives, my boys, were thrilled to see these white men doing this job 'properly'. So I when I told them that because of the navy launch having been fouled we had to do our stuff, they were delighted! It was amazing how smart they made themselves!

On the last day, we had to take the District Commissioner in his full dress uniform out to the Emerald. He went aboard, signalled goodbye to the Captain, and came away. We were instructed that the official drill was to approach the Emerald from the side at right angles and then moor up, and then when we left, when the District Commissioner re-embarked onto our launch, he was to stand in the rear of it and the launch should go at right angles away from the side for a certain distance. This was fine; we did this and, our boys, we really were smart! They really did do their stuff! I was thoroughly proud of them because this was something they'd never had before, never seen it before and they did it themselves – we didn't drill them in it, they did it themselves. The only snag was that after we picked up the District Commissioner to bring him off, he stood in the rear of the big launch facing the ship and we went off at right angles, and when we got about fifty yards away from the vessel, they fired a salute! We hadn't told our boys, well we didn't know, so we didn't warn our native boys that this was going to happen, and we nearly had a panic! They jumped out of their skins! They didn't know what was going on. Well I didn't either, but I knew what it was, but they nearly jumped out of their skins. But they recovered very well, and I was very pleased.

In the couple of days that the Emerald was moored in Lindi, apart from them coming ashore to see what facilities were available ashore, we were invited, a number of people - I think it finished up probably as all the white population of Lindi - were invited on board the vessel, and we were entertained on board the vessel. I had a long chat with the pilot of the craft that brought the mail. He was a very interesting chap to talk to, and told me many stories.

Native dances and customs

One of the experiences that I found extremely interesting was visiting the native villages around. Occasionally somebody, one of the senior officials, used to get an invitation from the village chief to visit them on a night when they were celebrating. Providing you went only with the invitation of the chief (and naturally you paid your respects to the village chief when you first arrived), you could get along very well indeed with the various villages.

Always on these occasions when you were invited there was a dance. Now, a dance was called *ngoma*, the *ngoma* being also the word for a drum, and it was really quite a fascinating evening to attend one of these *ngomas*. To start with, the drums had to be tuned. Now they were native-made drums and they were anything from something that looked as small as a large mug right up to a great big thing that stood on its end and was about four feet high and at least eighteen inches across. They were all made of wood, carved out of bits of tree. The vellum was not vellum, of course, it was just skin stretched across and sealed. They didn't have nails or anything like that, they bound the skin from the top, down underneath and back up the other side so it was held by a cord from one side of the circumference to the opposite side; they got many cords lashing this down and holding it and really getting it absolutely beautifully tight. The cords going round the wooden part of the drum really made a very interesting feature and some of them were decorated and really were delightful works of art.

The only method to tune these drums was to hold them near a heat source, usually the village fire. To hear them putting the drum skin over the top of the fire and then tapping it to hear what it was like, anything from the high notes from the little ones right down to the very deep booms of the great big large ones, was quite fascinating. You started wondering what pitch each drum is supposed to be. They know what pitch they want for their particular drum, but from a European point of view, you had no idea whether it was tuned right or wrong. All you knew was, once they started playing and got into their real rhythm, it was right! Not only was it delightful, not only the dance, the womenfolk of the tribe, they assembled and went round shuffling and shuffling and stamping and shuffling, and some of them starting singing and others came in with choruses, and all against the rhythm of these drums, the incessant regular rhythm of these drums.

Some of them played sort of freely, not a variation in tune as there was no tune, they had to stay as they were tuned. After a while it was really, rather hypnotic. You soon found not only were you nodding your head and swaying your body, and equally could be stamping your feet, but the whole of you was taken over by this, rather, I'd say insidious, but isn't meant as a nasty indication, it wasn't, it was really a fascinating system that gets right into you. You can quite understand how it is that some of the natives used to get really worked up and excited.

There were about four or five villages that we visited during the time I was in Lindi. Each of the villages was slightly different, but they were all based on the same principle, the chief of the village and the elders looked after the running of the village, and the women looked after the cleanliness of the village and it was really a well organised and thoroughly acceptable way of life for people who, to begin with start off with, really, absolutely nothing.

Until you get that thinking into your own mind, you cannot start to understand them. They have nothing, full stop. They have no knives and forks, no clothes; they've got no shoes, no drinking cups. They have nothing. They have a source of water because that's how they found that, amongst the tribe, and they find things to eat, whether they grow them themselves or they kill them, or whether it's something growing in the woodland that they scrub round for themselves; they find things to eat, but of themselves they have actually nothing. And anything they get they slowly acquire through their lifetime.

Even such a silly thing like a knife. You say, alright well you just go down the shop to buy it, but they don't have any money. They can't buy it, there's no such thing as money in their village. They have nothing. And if they want something that someone else has got they have to swap for what they want by giving away something they've got. But they've got so few things, they've got no riches amongst them. That's why when people talk about the native women who have several strings of beads given to them by their husbands or boyfriends or something, this is a great wealth to the woman, to have a string of beads given to her. After all, she started with absolutely nothing. The fact that she's working in the tribal village she works because that is the way to live. She doesn't earn money by doing work in the tribe, she lives by doing jobs that are necessary to be done in the village.

You quickly learn that there are certain things that you don't throw away as we would in this country. You know, just a silly thing like a tin. Obviously, we have lots of things we're used to getting in tins. You take the tin lid off, throw the lid away only a bit of tin, empty tin, wash it out, throw it away, only a bit of tin, but oh no, you don't do that there. What is it, a tin lid, that's nice and shiny that can make all sorts of things. Not only can you have the equivalent of a mirror, a reflector, you can also bend it over and make it into a very nice cutting tool. And the tin itself, it's a lovely thing because here you have something you can drink out of;

though it is very light to carry around, but equally if you drop it, it doesn't break, not like a gourd might. I know a gourd grows in the bush and after you've eaten the fruit out of the gourd you can dry it and carry fluid in but that can be dropped and broken quite easily. But a tin, no that's much better. It starts off being of use until it rusts, and you don't let it rust, you use it and see that you dry it afterwards. And then you start remembering that the native in Africa starts off in the bush with nothing. You soon learn, you realise, not to throw things away.

There's a whole storybook if anyone could get round to it, of markings, male and female, in native tribes: the facial markings; the cicatrices that they cut into themselves and rub ash into to make them swell; all sorts of facial and body markings that you and I would probably call disfigurement, but then it isn't, it's a case of enhancing their beauty. Even to the extent of filing their teeth. It must be the most agonising thing for the kids to have done, but for young girls in certain tribes it is the height of beauty to have filed teeth so that they are all pointed.

But there are equally some customs which are basic hygiene. I wondered first why the first duty of the woman of the hut, when she comes out of the hut first thing in the morning, was to sweep around the hut for about a metre and a half. Generally speaking, people say, this is one of the superstitions that they have, they sweep away the spirits. It isn't nonsense at all! During the night, the warmest part of the camp is in the hut. So during the night, the insects get comparatively cool compared with the warmth of the day, so look for the warmth they can find and they go towards the hut. Therefore in the morning, if you want to keep your hut clean and tidy and not have any bugs in it, first thing you do is to go around and sweep down the outside wall and sweep away from the hut to get rid of all the insects which have come to the hut during the night.

Building their huts also has certain customs and habits. There are all sorts of things depending on what type of hut is being built; if it's in an area where you have a mud wall, or whether it's just wickerwork made out of sticks and shrubs. A really basic one that I remember, amongst all the tribes is the tradition that once all the walls have been made and a little door left, before the roof is put on it's announced amongst the village that they've got everything ready to put the roof on. Then the day is announced for roofing and everyone in the village comes along and helps to put that roof on, because the roof, the inside of the house, must be covered over within the day before the dark comes. So from that dawn to dusk is the time when the roof must be fully completed on the new hut. Of course, those huts don't have any smoke holes like the Red Indian tepees because they don't have fires inside their huts, well certainly none of the ones I ran into, they might do in the mountainous areas, in Ubangi or places like that. But in the areas I knew, they never had fires in their huts, they always had their fires outside and they cooked outside in the open air. But that being the case, of course, there were no openings except the initial door and that door was only half as high as the perimeter wall. So that if you went in you either had to duck very low or you just had to crawl in. So going into a native hut for me was a bit of a problem because I literally had to get down on my hands and knees!

It's rather interesting that one time I was told by one of the Public Works Department (PWD) people, not in the Lindi district but somewhere else, when we were talking about accommodation and things like that, this PWD bloke was saying that they were extending a road and in order to house the workers they had to build huts in certain places. There were plans that were sent out from London that were approved, not only by whoever it was that sent the plans out but also approved by the 'do good' people who had to see that 'the black people didn't suffer and had good conditions to live in'. Well this was fine, and in due course the huts were built and they started using the road and they got to this area where next night they would be moving into these new huts. But the workers said, oh, no, no-no! They wouldn't go. After a long discussion it was discovered that they wouldn't go in because all these huts had got spaces for windows! No, a native hut can't possibly have windows so that the bad spirits can look in during the night! They must be completely, like their native kraals, completely enclosed with no opening except for their door, and that is covered over at night time. So you've got these beautiful buildings put up and approved that were absolutely useless and wasted because the boys just never would sleep in those huts, because they were built with places for the evil spirits to get in, and they had obviously got in before the roof was put on.

Leaving songs

After twelve months in Lindi I got notice to move. I handed over the station to D R F Lloyd and I gave the usual sort of going-away party. It was with great regret that I left Lindi. Apart from the fact that having gone down there when it was nothing, except a very small port with at most a dozen Europeans and maybe a couple of dozen Indians there; I left it with such happy memories. Everybody seemed to be friendly. It wasn't a case of it was all right for the first week or so and then everybody got upset with each other. Nobody had seemed to have got upset with anybody over the whole period that I was there. It was happy, and I really learnt how to have a happy station, a happy area, right out in the bush where you didn't have much, you imported everything if you wanted it, you made fun for yourself. The only way to run a radio was to take a battery out of your car and attach it to your radio as there was no such thing as electricity, everything was run by paraffin if you wanted lights. Even our fridge was run on paraffin. But the folks were all friendly, I learnt an awful lot in those eighteen months down there, not only about getting on with people and various senior people but also with the farmers up country and particularly with the local natives. I really thoroughly enjoyed it and was very sad to have to leave. But on the other hand I'd had malaria on six different occasions, and I really shouldn't have stayed any longer in case I continued to get malaria as I did then.

Talking about saying goodbye reminds me of a couple of native songs that seemed to be appropriate. There was one that the natives sang any time they were doing routine work like rowing or hauling or something. It started off with the two words 'Johnny mbaya' which virtually means 'bad Johnny' or 'naughty Johnny'. But I was never able to catch any of the following verses, they seemed to make up the verses as they went along and then came in with the chorus. You noticed very frequently when we were working that one of them would look up at you and obviously he was singing a verse which made up a story about you, and the others would roar with laughter and come in with the chorus which started 'Johnny mbaya'. The other one was a little sentimental ditty that seemed to have been sung by the Europeans at Lindi when any of their members was going home on leave, because they only went on leave every two and a half years, then they had three months leave in the UK. So that when they went they didn't know whether they would be coming back, it depended on the Colonial administration. And so frequently you would hear this song sung from the jetty as the boat took the resident out to the steamer. It was called, well it was introduced by 'Kwaheri,' which was a greeting, well the opposite of a greeting, a cheerio-goodbye sort of thing, and this song was very like the song made famous by Vera Lynn - 'wish me luck as you wave me goodbye'.

The one we had down in Lindi started off 'Kwaheri - goodbye, I'm going off to my homeland now. I don't know whether I'll be coming back but remember me and if I do come back I'll see you again.'

Chapter 8:
Butiaba

Geoffrey left Lindi on 3rd June 1938 and went up to Nairobi, spending a short time doing an anti-malarial course, although he never mentioned he had trouble with malaria to his family and did not suffer from it later on, thank goodness.

It was a new thing that the medicos had found out and it meant taking atabrine for several days then quinine for several days. You had to go on continuously and if one of them turned your eyeballs yellow, you had to stop; if the other one turned your eyeballs purple, you had to stop, and so on. Fortunately, I went through the whole course and never had malaria afterwards, despite living for another three years in malarial areas.

His short stay in Nairobi was good for relaxation among more Airways people and 'civilians' than he'd seen for months. His next posting (in June 1938) was over to Butiaba (on the north-facing coast of Lake Albert), which was really an emergency landing area between Malakal in the Sudan and Port Bell in Uganda. It was unsuitable as a halfway point of the route down to South Africa all the way down from Cairo; it made Malakal to Kampala one of the longest hops and therefore could take the least load. It was best as an emergency bolthole. Geoffrey undertook that posting on the basis that Butiaba was going to close and the facilities moved somewhere else, but where was yet to be decided.

I knew nothing about Butiaba, but then I knew nothing about Lindi before I got there. I flew up to Port Bell and from there I was driven by the Station Superintendent from Kampala over to Butiaba, and left to get on with it!

There was no station superintendent at Butiaba that I took over from. The facilities were limited to a mooring, a motor boat, and a radio station. That was it! There was me in charge and we had a coxswain and a radio operator. We all lived up at the Government rest-house, Bukumi camp. It was right on the main, well, the only road, but I remember it was on the top of the escarpment. You had a winding road going down the escarpment to the plains beneath; these were the plains in which lay Lake Albert and Lake Tanganyika and Lake Edward and those lakes that lay in part of the Rift Valley.

It was fortunate that the radio operator there was South African; he had with him not only his complete kit but also his cook and personal boy. That meant we had someone who could cook for us because neither the coxswain nor I had any permanent servants and there were none available round that camp. The camp was four or five miles away from the port of Butiaba and the only thing between us and Butiaba apart from one small kraal, was bush. All sorts of antelopes of course, but also buffaloes, elephants, lions, the complete range of the usual East African animals, plus an awful lot of baboons!

The journey from Bukumi camp down the escarpment then across the plain to Butiaba harbour could be quite exciting. On one occasion, we were going down and suddenly found there was a whole mob of baboons in the way. Well, you can ease down into a mob of baboons, but they wouldn't take much notice of you. I got out of the car, picked up a rock and threw it at them to get them out of the road. One didn't do any good, so I picked up another stone and threw that one, and a little while later I found that they were picking up stones and throwing them at us! I learnt my lesson there: with a baboon you never throw stones at it or anything like that because they copy you, and they become quite accurate!

At the office

We had a little office in the actual port of Butiaba; it was an official port, because it was the base for the *SS Corynton* and the river steamer *Lugard*. The only other people there were a superintendent - he was a Scotsman, as was the norm, but he had his wife and his daughter with him which was very unusual indeed – and one or two Sikh engineers servicing the boats. The boats operated around Lake Albert, across to the Congo and back and up and down. They were part of the Kenya-Uganda Railways and Harbours Company (KURH), a Government organisation.

The little office that we had was quite small, it just had the absolute necessities, a little store of engineering spares and the radio station for the radio operator. I particularly remember that station because the first thing that happened when we went down to the office was to get the bush boys to bring up a bucket of water. This water was straight out of the lake. First you strained it through wire mesh, then you strained it through linen, and then you put it into a pot and boiled it, and after you'd boiled it you strained it through some very fine cotton mesh; then you put it into a great big filter, which looked like it had chalk candles in it. What was it called, a Higginson or Hutchinson candles or filters? It was only after the water dripped through these filter candles that you were able to boil it again and have a cup of tea!

The other thing was the transport. We had there the Ford V8 station wagon, which was the established vehicle for Imperial Airways in outstations. I'd never met it before because we didn't have one down in Lindi, and the ones in Nairobi were more sophisticated. You had more of a town there, more built-up roads, whereas out in Butiaba it was just a gravel track made by trucks which kept them rolled down. They were very wearing on tyres and very uneven surfaces, but there was one part that was a nice straight stretch. One time, just for devilment, we tried to see what speed we could get up on this. It was the first time I had driven a motorcar at just over 60 mph (96 kph) and boy, was that a rough journey!

Fishing

A couple more people were there because of an oil rig. They were doing exploratory drilling about a mile inland from the harbour. I don't remember which company it was now, but two or three of the drillers were quite friendly and we used to entertain them frequently up at the Bukumi camp. One of them, a Pole, was very keen on fishing. He was delighted because we'd got our motor launch and were quite happy to take him out fishing, not only in the evening time but also on his days off - provided we could wangle the petrol. While I was there, I got quite keen on fishing, particularly because we had the Nile perch in that area. This was a reasonable size fish, in fact any fish under 5 lbs we threw back in the water. They were real good fish, and quite big fish, so that I enjoyed my fishing because of meeting these blokes from the oil exploration place.

You had to be careful because you might pick up some other sort of fish; there was the *ngege* and the *ngasa* as well as the *mbuta*. It was the *mbuta* that was useful for eating, the others were a bit bony, a bit rough. But a reasonable size Nile perch or the *mbuta* which we caught, not less than 5 lbs weight, we used to take back up to the camp, because the radio operator's cook was very good with them. He gutted the fish and rubbed salt into it both front and back, and then put it up onto a sort of staging up in the air about three feet off the ground, which was made by sticks lashed together. Underneath he made a fire, which was smoky from the wood he always used to use, so that we got our fish, not only dried and salted but also smoked. It might sound horrible, but when it was cooked, it really was the most tasty fish. And having not had anything like that for years, I really thoroughly enjoyed it. So apart from the inevitable meat that we shot - we didn't have any chicken, it was always shoot your own meat - the fish came in as a really delightful change.

There is a series of labelled photographs in Geoffrey's archives, showing flying boat Canopus *ADHL arriving Butiaba during a 'proving flight' in March 1938. Geoffrey did not arrive at Butiaba until June, but the notes on the back of the photos are in his writing, although they are numbered sequentially in someone else's hand. On one of them* Canopus *is called "Pawpuss". How many other 'boats had appropriate nicknames?*
There is a close-up labelled "W/O Paddy ....". This must be Paddy Coussans, standing in the nose area having picked up the mooring. This 'proving flight' must have been to prove Butiaba was operational, since Canopus *was the first Short C Class (S23) to be delivered (1936).*

Chapter 9:
Have station, will travel

The orders came through to move the station from Butiaba up to Juba, which was then a small town in the Sudan. The alternative had been a place called Laropi. Geoffrey had seen the survey done by Bill Linstead, read his notes and plans and there was just nothing there.

In a way, setting up Lindi was a piece of cake compared to moving the station. Geoffrey had to make most of the arrangements himself; some bookings of regional transport were made by either HQ Nairobi or HQ Cairo, since Geoffrey was crossing borders. The Central African and the Middle East areas had their boundaries contingent with the northern border of Uganda and the southern border of Sudan. He can tell the story himself, but note that he tended to say up the river, or up the Nile, when he was talking about going north, i.e. downstream, towards Juba, Khartoum and eventually to Egypt. This has been corrected as far as possible.

The planned route up to Juba was from Butiaba across Lake Albert, to the water going out of Albert into the Albert Nile. Then it went up the Albert Nile to Nimule, then from Nimule by road, because north of Nimule you've got a lot of rapids so no boats go up there; so after Nimule we had to transfer onto land and go up to Juba.

We were given a date when we should move and, as the skipper of the *Corynton* and the marine superintendent both lived in Butiaba, we were able to get ourselves co-ordinated and booked for the journey. It was an interesting exercise because we had a lot of equipment to move. There was the usual sort of office equipment and radio pack set, the station car, and the stairs, but also there were the two launches, the passenger launch and the patrol launch. There were the night flares, six, eight of those, and we also needed to take up our Shell barge. Now the Shell barge is no lightweight job. It is all steel and contains thousands of gallons of fuel. It is operated by a diesel engine and it really is a solid chunk of metal. We got all this stuff organised on barges or on tow, and it was taken from Butiaba up to the river mouth by *SS Corynton*; the barges and the launches were towed behind, I've got a photograph of the long tow that was behind the *SS Corynton*.

When we got to the river mouth, it was a case of 'all change'. The *SS Corynton* couldn't operate up further because of the underwater reeds and so on, so we had to transfer to the *SS Lugard*. That was a stern wheeler, like the Mississippi stern wheeler. This meant we had to modify our loading; the boats couldn't be towed so everything had to be either taken on board the *Lugard* or lashed alongside. The *Lugard* burnt wood fuel, so we had to have stopping stations or refuelling halts where there were stacks of timber cut to size that could be loaded in the space that the *Lugard* had for them. We kept stopping and loading with fuel, but it was noticeable that it became less and less available locally and more and more had to be bought from further up country. The operation had been going on for quite some time and the timber anywhere near the river had already been chopped and collected by the steamer. Now it had to be collected further and further from the river. This was one of the tragedies of the developments in Africa but there was no other fuel and you had to have fuel, you couldn't use wind, not trying to travel down the Nile.

We did pass and see the river that comes from Jinja where the water tumbled out of Lake Victoria, goes up north and round and comes out via the Murchison Falls. Then it tumbles into the north of Lake Albert, and then out again of Lake Albert into the Albert Nile and continues the beautiful and marvellous waterway that is the Nile.

It was quite fascinating because the river was wandering about all over the place, and the growth of waterweed and reeds and the Nile cabbage, and every sort of greenery was there. We repeatedly ran "aground" because we were sitting on this growth of reed. The skipper was perfectly happy because he'd done this journey regularly; I think they did it once a month up to Nimule and back again. It was part of the organisation of transport, organisation all the way from Cape Town up to Cairo by all sorts of means, none of which meant flying, because previously there would have been no aeroplanes in the area.

Nimule

After about three days, we reached Nimule. We had to tie up and start the palaver of taking everything out of the boats, barges and the water and moving it onto land.

Somewhere the arrangements made between the regional headquarters of Middle East and Central Africa went wrong. On arrival at Nimule we found there was no transport, no connection to meet us. We had to carry on and release the steamer to go back south, but we had nowhere to live, nothing to eat, nothing. Not even a sheet or blanket to cover us over, because that was the way we travelled. There was a Government rest-house at Nimule of course; this was really a roof with mosquito proofing all the way round, and inside there were the usual thongs stretched across four posts which was your bed. It anticipated you had your mattress, sheets and blankets with you, which the government officials normally had, when they went travelling.

So there we were, stuck. We hoped the connection from Juba really was coming to Nimule, to pick us up, to transport the passenger launch, the patrol launch and of course the Shell barge. We didn't know when it was going to arrive, so we did a deal with the captain of the steamer. He gave us some food and some water, and some bottles of beer, and a couple of blankets, sufficient for us to be able to last us for twenty-four hours, in the hope that we would be picked up in that time. Of course, the skipper had no authority to pass over equipment from a KURH steamer to strangers like us, but he knew our contract had been made at his headquarters in Nairobi. He was a good fellow and he let us 'borrow' these things. We promised to arrange for the stuff to be there for him to pick up on his next trip, which would of course be in a month's time, and he got us to sign for these and said 'ok, then, well best of luck and I hope you enjoy your stay in Nimule if you don't get to Juba!' Then when he was refuelled and unloaded, he cast off, turned round and went south.

The coxswain, who was called Springer - I never knew his Christian name - and the radio operator (I don't remember him because he was an 'odd' character), we just arranged to look after ourselves, and our crews, in reasonable safety for the night. We had skeleton launch crews we were taking with us to Juba so we could use the boats until we'd recruited new local labour. We made arrangements for them as well, and hoped we could spend the night reasonably healthily, and that somebody would arrive the next day so that we could carry out the rest of the journey up to Juba which was another 110 miles. Nimule, being the northern most part of the Albert Nile that people could come to because of the cataracts north of there, was not a very healthy spot. In fact, malaria was rife, yellow fever was rife, and of course bilharzias was in the water, so you daren't bathe or anything like that. Any water that was around you'd have to filter and boil and refilter, but we hadn't got that equipment with us, so we were really relying on what we had managed to buy from the skipper of the *Lugard*.

It was the middle of the next day before transport arrived, and this consisted of trucks with bogeys which were operated by a company called SHUN, which actually meant Societé Haut-ouiae de Nil which was technically a Belgian company but it operated both sides of the Sudan-Uganda border; they were a very useful transporting company. Also with them were the two station wagons from the Sudan railways who came through, both with native drivers, and they were expecting to pick us up. Why they arrived twenty-four hours afterwards I never did find out, nobody seemed to know; it just happened that way and we were the ones to get caught.

I had a long discussion with the SHUN man about transporting the launches and the barge, because the road from Nimule to Juba was over 110 miles and you could only anticipate the transport that was carrying these very heavy marine items to be moved about four miles an hour at the very best - that was provided there were no heavy rains for the next three or so days. It would certainly take them a couple of days to get the launches and the barges out of the water onto their trolleys. They had to make up their trolleys with independent bogeys and then get in logs between them to space the bogeys away from the prime mover and have them sufficiently strong to have the launch and the Shell barge to sit on. Most worrying, of course, was the Shell barge. That was the heaviest of the lot, and it really was solid. Anyway the SHUN representative was reasonably happy about it, and I went off to Juba with the other two staff members and what I could get into the two station wagons, leaving the SHUN man to deliver the equipment up into Juba as early as he could – which of course was the contract, so I wasn't doing anything I shouldn't have done.

We arrived on the road up from Nimule only to find ourselves on the other side of the river from the town of Juba. It was a very small place at that time. So the final step was the ferry. That ferry consisted of a cold-starting diesel because you had to warm up the cylinder head with a blow-lamp before you could turn the starting handle to get the cylinder to fire. That was lashed to a rather large iron barge, flat, so that you rolled down the side of the bank onto this flat iron barge, and then when the engine was warm enough and the skipper of the boat could make it go, you started chugging across the river.

This was really the first time I recognised the problem of crossing the Nile from bank to bank. Here the river was running at least five knots, and this was the low season, not the high season when you would get much higher speeds. All the time you had to reckon, you could never go across, you had to go up and back or else you landed further down the river than where you started. The introduction to this thought of using the current and the engine in a boat was something new to me, and I was glad I learnt it on my first day.

We went up to the Juba Hotel, because there was nowhere else we could possibly go, and it was actually a very pleasant hotel.

Chapter 10:
Juba and the Rejaf station

Having had the experience of starting a station from nothing at Lindi, it was not too hard for Geoffrey, opening up Juba as a flying boat base. There was already a runway for land planes less than a mile away from the Juba hotel, and from the hotel you could see the planes on the runway when they were landing; there weren't very many coming through in those days. The required stretch of water was not so close to hand, though.

    I had of course to start my normal drill, the first of which was to call on the senior Government official, who happened to be the Governor of the Equatorial Province. He was an important man of course, as he was completely in charge of Equatoria. It must have been 20,000 square miles; a lot of it was bush, some of it was swamp and there were very few white people there, but of course quite a lot of natives who at that time we would call 'quite primitive', in fact many of them were very primitive. It was a very interesting station from that point of view to see the African natives and their way of living. Anything and everything they wanted had to come out of the flora and fauna of the area.

    The Governor was Martin Parr, and of course, other than the Indian merchants, I was the only 'civilian' there, a civilian on the basis that I didn't work for the Sudan Government. All the other British people were members of the Sudan Government Civil Service and as such became underlings of the Governor. So I was in a somewhat unique position; a white man who had no responsibility to the Governor except from a political point of view. He couldn't order me to do anything unless I was doing something against the law, and he couldn't instruct me to do something unless I thought it was a good thing to do in relation to Imperial Airways. In fact we started off on a slightly difficult footing because of his lack of conception of having an Englishman that was not on his staff.

Bush-whacking to Rejaf

The local PWD man (Public Works Department) had some idea where the survey for the flying boat alighting area had been made, and although there were no charts left, he gave me a good idea of where it was and also the difficulty of getting up there by launch. It would be going against the flow of the Nile to go from Juba up to the beach at Rejaf; there were many cataracts on the waterway and it was a very hazardous thing to do. With our patrol launch - it was 100 horsepower engine in this patrol launch so she was a nice handy and powerful unit - we tried to go upstream against the current and the cataracts, but we found it was far too dangerous. The last thing we wanted to do was to shear off our underwater gear, because it was impossible to mend it ourselves and we would have to wait for spare parts coming out from the UK if we did get into trouble.

We abandoned that idea and we tried to find it instead by going over the country. This meant we had to get the car over the river; we crossed the Nile, from the west bank to the east, by the routine ferry and went down by the Nimule road. There was what they used to call a mountain (but it was only about 500 feet high), but it was really conical with practically flat land around it. If you could see over the woodland, or scrubland, you could spot this distinctive hill for miles and miles around. Going down the Nimule road, we hoped to be able to see this conical hill out to the west, then decide exactly where and how we would cut into this bush to get to the reach that had been surveyed, at a place called Rejaf.

The place we thought would be best to go in towards the reach really was tough bush country, and there were problems here that I didn't know how to overcome. I had a chat with the PWD man and he suggested I talk to the local prison superintendent. Many of the prisoners in the prison camp were officially in there doing hard labour. The prison superintendent had nothing whatsoever for them to do in the way of hard labour. The PWD man suggested I see if he would let us have a couple of hard labour prisoners with pangas and an armed guard (they had to have that of course) and use them to try and cut a track through for us to go to the river. So I had a chat with the police superintendent. He was delighted. His only conditions were that I provided the transport for the two prisoners and the guard and saw that they had adequate food and water for their day, and they came back, of course - safely and at the proper time! He was delighted and I wouldn't have to pay a penny for them.

So we went down the road, stopped where we thought we might be able to find a way through, and with the help of the two prisoners slashing with their pangas we started clearing the path in. It was quite amusing, the relationship between the guard and the prisoners was quite good, and we found in the end that we had quite an amusing time; there were no problems, no troubles at all. All of us were working, trying to do the same thing; they did the hard work with their pangas chopping and we stomped the stuff down and carried on trying to get through.

After a while, we came to rather swampy ground. This water had flooded into the countryside when the Nile was high, and had not seeped back into the Nile through the slightly higher banks. So this gave us a problem, and we weren't quite certain how to overcome it.

There were one or two local natives, they just appeared, who came to see what we were doing: they were interested spectators. I got the police guard man to talk to them, and discovered that there was a lot of water between here and the river, but the easiest thing would be to go down a hippo run! Well, I didn't know what a hippo run was in those days, I'd never been in hippo country before except in the high bush around Nairobi. The locals very kindly scouted around in this wet earth and muddy place and then came across what was virtually a tunnel through the fifteen foot high elephant grass. It was a run that the hippos used when they came out of the Nile and went wandering round the countryside. They kept their feet as dry as they could, and they pressed down all the greenery there was, so it was reasonably firm footing to be able to follow that.

After a few days work, we almost fell into the Nile over the banks to find this dirty muddy river flowing along at about five knots from south to north in front of us! There was no clearing on the side, so we then had to start chopping down the elephant grass around us so we had somewhere reasonable that we could sit down, yes, we did sit down because that part was slightly higher than the surrounding country, so that part was dry. We had arrived!

Setting up Rejaf station

We looked at the river and saw a reasonably straight stretch of swirling water that didn't seem any width at all, but it was a straight stretch; it looked like the real one and the only one we'd be able to find. I hoped we had achieved our objective, and I went back to the hotel having felt that we'd done our job.

But there were still many problems to overcome to make it possible to get through from the road to the reach.

We would want transport to and from, because if it were going to be an airport we'd have to have Customs there. We'd want fuel there, and of course *we* wanted to be there and we wanted to be able to put up our own little radio station. Well, the little radio station would be in the launch, but we had to get the big passenger launch up there as well, quite apart from getting the patrol launch up there. There was also the Shell barge to transport too.

Geoffrey pressed on with clearing the site, using the prisoners with the prison escort. The low ground between the riverbank and the Nile meant they had to build a road! While that was going on Geoffrey arranged for a couple of sedan chairs to be made so that he and the coxswain could get through the swampy area hoisted on the boys' shoulders. He comments "Really colonial stuff that!"

It was a difficult job getting the Rejaf landing area surveyed and it all had to be done using very basic instruments – feet.

We were able to clear a narrow bit along the east bank of the Nile so that I was able to put in stakes down the side and get a reasonably accurate measurement of the length. Pace it out, put a stake in to mark one hundred yards and pace it out again and put another stake in for another hundred yards. Working out what the width of the river was, and the bank the other side, presented even more problems. It was almost impossible to get up the opposite bank because of the terrain, the water, the swamps and the general bush. Fortunately I remembered my schooldays and, as I'd got my prismatic compass with me, I was able to do the odd a bearing here and a bearing there, with my baseline along the east bank of the river. Then I calculated reasonably well how wide the river was on that stretch.

Now we had access, but we still hadn't solved the problem of getting the launches between the road and the river. This was really solved for us. One day when we went down there, we found that not only were the swamps between the road and the river much deeper, but also the river had risen a lot. This indicated that the small rains had occurred up in Uganda and the Congo and it was possible that with the river rising, we might be able to get the small launch, the passenger launch and even the Shell barge up the river from Juba over what had previously been impassable rapids. On a suitable time and day, with great effort and trepidation, we set out with the patrol launch only, up the river to see if we could find a deep enough channel up to Rejaf. After much shoving and pushing and worrying and sweating we were able to get the patrol launch up into the reach. We were very pleased with this, and as the river was still rising, we were able to bring up the passenger launch the next day. The Shell man followed our example and brought his Shell barge up from the ferry, where it had been standing all the time waiting to be put into the river up at Rejaf.

Geoffrey was very thankful to end the day with all three launches up at the reach and moored reasonably well to avoid any damage from floating debris coming down on the flood of the river. But having got there by launch and having sent the cars up the road to meet them, they got their feet wet walking through the swamp from the reach to the road!

The next big problem in establishing the station was to get the moorings laid. According to official instructions, moorings had one-ton clump anchors and yards of half-inch stud link chain, and a cubic metre of concrete as a sinker below the rising chain up to the buoy. There were supposed to be two of them linked by a chain, at such a distance so that you could have two flying boats swinging at anchor and they wouldn't bash their tails together.

The reach was not big enough for this layout. Getting a couple of cubic metres of concrete somewhere up there and being able to float them and then drop them into the reach, with a one ton clump anchor and stud link chain, this was quite impossible! We had no facilities, the only way we could get up the river was over the rapids, and we certainly hadn't got any lighters or anything like that we could hold these things on or pay them out from. So, we just had to say "we laid the moorings". I must admit they not laid down as specified, not only that but instead of laying a plot of two, I decided I would have one at the north end of the reach and one at the south end of the reach. These would be just clear of the sandbanks that really denoted the operational limits of the reach suitable for the flying boats.

It was at this time that we had our radio operator sent down to us by the Middle East Region, who naturally flew down via Malakal and picked up the Sudan Railway steamer on to Juba. Up till then we only had the use of the Marconi radio station in Juba, which was ordinary normal telegraphic communication. We now had our own station at Rejaf, equipped in the launch, and a knowledgeable operator trained to use it.

For our terminal, we erected a conical thatched roof based on four posts stuck in the ground. That meant we had somewhere rainproof when it did rain, other than in the launches, and we had somewhere to stand in the shade when we were waiting for aircraft.

So when we sent off our signal to the Middle East Headquarters saying 'we can now receive and handle flying boats in Rejaf', it hid the reality of the operation. To meet our flying boats we had to leave Juba in the morning, drive down to the ferry, drive our cars onto the ferry boat to get across to the other side, and drive down to the point where we got off the road. Then we walked from the road through the track that we'd cut to Rejaf, being carried over the wet bits in our sedan chairs, and what's more, the Customs officer had to do this too.

Whatever the weather

According to the book, we had responsibility to contact an incoming flying boat to find out how the plane was doing and give him a local weather update so that he knew what the conditions were, and then we had to put up a windsock. Well this was crazy, a windsock? You can't go putting up a thing like that! So what we did is got the boys to put together some rubbish, light a fire, put some wet grass on the top of it, and it was a lovely indicator of which way the winds were. Far, far better than having to fiddle with a windsock and probably losing it overnight anyway.

Although it was primitive, to say the least, we were in a position to handle the first flight (*probably* Corinna *G-AEUC*), and the skipper, one of the experienced skippers, was very pleased with the set-up.

The only problem was being very short of weather station information about Rejaf. Well of course, there was no reporting station or anything like that up there, apart from reports given by me. From then on, on the mornings of the aircraft arrival, I used to go out and have a look around and make my weather report up, and pass it on to the Government radio station, the Marconi communications station, who would then relay it up to Khartoum and Malakal to be passed on to the aircraft. It was fortunate that I'd done that Met course when I was up at Croydon, because I was familiar with the observations necessary and also with the code indications, so I could send off the message with adequate information on the weather in a ten letter code.

This procedure was repeated down to Kampala when the flying boats were leaving northbound from that station. Subsequently when our radio at the base in Rejaf was working well we could give actual weathers to the aircraft an hour or so before they landed.

One day, there was a northbound flying boat due, I woke up in Juba and the rain was pouring down! It was absolutely sheeting down, you couldn't see anywhere because of the storm. There was no wind, it was just coming down in bucket-loads. So I thought I'd better warn the aircraft and I wrote up my warning message, in plain language but I gave it the unusual prefix of XXX. When I got down to the Marconi station in Juba and said I wanted it sent off urgently to the aircraft, which by that time had just left Port Bell. He said, ooh, he couldn't send off a XXX, that was set as terrible priority. I said, yes and if you want authority I'll give you the authority, you just send that off. So he sent it and within three or four minutes we got a reply from the aircraft, asking for information on the direction the storm had arrived from. Of course, I just didn't know, I woke just when the weather was hitting us and hadn't seen where it came from. There was no apparent movement, the rain was just tumbling down. It was most unfortunate but at least I said I couldn't do it, my answer was just a terse one 'Unable to observe.' And I left it at that.

When the aircraft got in, the skipper was able to look out for the weather and see the storm and which way it was moving so he could come in behind it. And that in fact is what he did. But if he hadn't have been able to find it he could have aborted back to Butiaba, so I'd done the right thing. But he said that in future if those conditions arrived, if I could find which direction the storm was travelling, it would have helped them because they wouldn't then have to search around to find out which direction to get behind it. So, you know, even with that I learned something.

Elephants

Certainly when we established Rejaf the biggest problem was getting down there. The Government started the clearance of the track between the road and the river, and slowly that was cleared and slowly they started building it up. Well they had to build it up, to get it up to the level of the swamp, and over the swamp, so theoretically it wouldn't be flooded when the Nile flooded. But I recall during that period the number of times that although the road was built up fairly well, you'd come down in the morning and find great big breaches in the banks where the elephants had gone through overnight. They'd just stamped it around and stamped it around, so that what should have been an embankment that carried the road was just flattened down again.

On the occasion when we did have a flood the water just rushed through the gap that they'd made and because of the rushing water it made the washing away of the road even more intense. So there was a lot of fun building that road. The road was done by the Public Works Department but they just used, as I had, the prisoners that had been sentenced to hard labour, and they were ferried down there regularly every day and they were just digging up the soil and dumping it. I know it sounds terrible, but it's not as hard, slavish, as it sounds. The baskets they filled they put on their heads, and carried it up and dumped it at the top, and they came back and got another few shovelfuls into the basket. It wasn't what anyone could really think of as 'slave labour' and because they were out in the air and doing something, instead of being in the prison compound doing absolutely nothing, the prisoners seemed to be a jolly happy crowd!

Eventually they got the road completed and then could drive all the way through: from Juba to the river, cross the river by ferry to the East bank, then down the main road to the turnoff, along the road and the embanked road through to the end at Rejaf. It finished up a slight embankment to the river, where they had the grass roof under which they later installed their telephone line. The two launches were moored in the river; the big launch, the passenger launch, was where the radio operator had his operations.

Land planes

Another part of my Imperial Airways duty was to look after any planes that came into the land planes area. This was quite fun, really. There weren't many that came through; they were mostly sporting light aeroplanes with somebody who wanted to fly somewhere that no-one had ever been, or they were trying to make their name by exploring certain parts of the country. In any case, they were all little things, I don't know what types now, but all high winged monoplanes with cabins big enough for, say, four people, but usually there were only maximum two in them, and the rest was for emergency equipment and extra tankage and so on. It was amusing when they came in, to look after them, put them in the hotel, arrange weathers for them, and get to know when and where they were going, and to do what one would normally do for a plane. It was a service that Imperial Airways carried out for any aeroplane belonging to another company that we had an arrangement with. Any private flyers, we picked them up, arranged for their petrol (we always charged it to their account, of course), fixed the hotel for them, and again, they would pay but we acted as an agency for any plane that landed at any of our airports.

I remember one occasion though, they were doing repairs to the aerodrome in Juba, and I got a message from the PWD people. They'd heard there was an aeroplane arriving in two or three days time, and they couldn't stop doing their repairs on the runway of the airport because they wanted to get them completed before the rainy season started. They didn't want to hold them up for this aeroplane and start again, so they wondered what they could do about it.

"Well, it looks all right to me," I said. "What are you doing?"

The PWD man said: "We're progressively going over the airport and resurfacing it."

"You'll always know where the surface is safe and isn't safe won't you?"

He said yes, so I said, "well, we'll mark it up."

"How do we do that?"

"Have you any A markers?" I asked.

"A markers? What's an A marker?"

So I sketched out what I knew:

In air terms it was a permanent thing that if you had that sort of construction going on, you put A markers along the edge of where the 'thumbs down' area was, so you marked which was the good land and which was the bad land. In the area that was bad you put a white cross. An aeroplane coming over would look down and see the normal outline of the runway (usually whitened bricks or something like that), and across a part of it there was this little structure, only about 18 inches off the ground and three feet wide, marked in white edges with a red stripe over the top of it, across the runway. On one side, there would be a white cross. He'd know he had to land in the part which didn't have the white cross but otherwise the other side of the A markers.

The PWD knocked them up quickly enough and painted them, and I showed them how the normal layout would be, and on the particular occasion when this aeroplane was due, they put them out and carried on working and then when the aeroplane was heard, they cleared the runway thinking, well, what's going to happen? They were absolutely amazed when the plane, without having been told, swooped over the runway and looked and came down and landed, just over the top of the A markers and touched down no trouble at all! The pilot of the aeroplane just accepted it as normal. They were surprised that anyone could interpret signs on the ground like that without being told about it. It quite amazed them!

Sabena

A big occasion for us was when Sabena, which was the Belgian airline, started a service from the west coast of the Congo through Congo stations to connect with the north-south airline at Juba. They then had a reasonable connection between the Congo and the French Equatorial Africa stations to South Africa and to the Middle East. They operated it with Lockheed 14s that they had out there, and the Sabena pilots who had been flying around in that area for some time had never got all joined up. It was a very amicable arrangement and as the Sabena pilots were used to Imperial Airways and I was used to these people when I was in Croydon, we worked together, had no troubles at all, in fact we got quite friendly with them and it was a very happy operation. They didn't have a lot of traffic, they brought some mail in which was put on the northbound or southbound flying boat. They occasionally had a passenger come through. Sometimes there were passengers on the west coast who couldn't get on the land plane service between Freetown and Khartoum, but they were willing to come round on the long journey down to Duala, Brazzaville, Leopoldville, Stanleyville, up to Juba and then from Juba up to Khartoum and the near East on the flying boat.

The fact that I spoke reasonable French was also a great help because most of those pilots didn't have a word of English and the people in Juba wouldn't have known what to do.

Chapter 11:
The *Corsair* Affair

One of the more infamous events in the Africa route's history involved the flying boat Corsair *G-ADVB. Geoffrey had numerous interviews about the event with journalists and authors; he is cited in various books. This is his version of the event, which differs in details from other accounts, including the official one.*

One big occasion was with *Corsair*, which was the flying boat coming up from Kampala, or rather, Port Bell, one day.

We were operating radio from Rejaf and our operator said to me "There's something gone wrong here because they're making extraordinary calls for DF bearings". [direction finding]

So I asked him to tell me what was going on, and later he said: "You know, they're completely lost, they don't know where they are. They can't seem to be able to get a decent bearing in order to be able to find out where they are. They've asked me to start transmitting Vs so they can get a bearing on us here, because they think they might be near enough to pick up my signals."

So he then starting keying the Vs, which is the code qsv, and he continued to qsv until his fingers got tired and there was still no answer, and then he asked me to take over! Well, he showed me how to do it, I did it for a while and left off, and he listened in to see if there was any answer or call, but nothing seemed to happen. The aircraft was way overdue.

I had already notified Port Bell in order to check up and find out what fuel it had so that I could see whether it might have to crash land because there was no fuel. But it seemed to be still flyable by the amount of fuel that was on board. I was told it had so many gallons off, in other words, it had a maximum load, but it hadn't taken full petrol in order to carry that maximum load. But his message actually read "50 gallons off **on paper**". That meant to us that although the [loading] paper showed he was 50 gallons short of a full tank and therefore the aircraft was not overloaded, in point of fact he'd still got those 50 gallons on. Officially, the aircraft was all right, but the station and I and the skipper would know it had taken off over load. It was not an amount that would make any real difference but it would be a technicality in the event of any official enquiry or something like that.

It was long overdue when we got a signal which was repeated to us, funnily enough, from Khartoum. It was routed Khartoum down to Juba Marconi station; Juba Marconi station called us and told us they'd received a message through Stanleyville saying the aircraft had landed on the River Dungu [Dangu] at a village called Faraje [Faradge] in the eastern Congo region, which was not too far from the town of Aba. Nobody was hurt but they wouldn't be able to get off, so that meant I would have to do something because I was obviously the nearest station.

So I packed up as quickly as I could at Rejaf because there were no other flying boats around, and we went back to Juba across the ferry back to the hotel, and there I wondered, well, what do we do now? I decided that the only thing to do was to go over there. So we loaded up our station wagon and I purloined, or borrowed, or whatever you like, one of the Sudan Railway station wagons which were part of the transport of the Juba Hotel. I told them I didn't want their driver, and my coxswain would do the driving on the second vehicle, because I didn't know where we'd get to, how we'd get on or anything. We just loaded up with extra petrol, a can of water - we always carried extra water around with us - a mosquito net, my shotgun, a spade and some food. I drove the front car and the coxswain drove the other one and we 'moved off' on our way to somewhere which we didn't know, but nevertheless we found it.

It was rather amusing, I read in a book which was meant to be the history of Imperial Airways and BOAC [Penrose], when they made reference to this landing out at Faradge, they made some comment about the place being 150 miles away from Juba which was the nearest civilised place:

"To Juba, the nearest point though over 150 miles away over roadless broken country."

If I remember rightly although it's a long time ago, of course, my road meter said 105 miles, and I never went through roadless broken country, there were fire tracks which led us, and we had no trouble getting there. So it sounds nice in a history book, doesn't it?

The track from Aba, the nearest settlement that we hit, was pretty ropey and rough, but that was the sort of bush country we went through. Even the one or two normal so-called civilised roads were only gravel tracks.

The skipper, John Alcock, had in fact had made all sorts of arrangements of his own for his passengers. From my point of view, I got organised to take all the passengers in the two station wagons that we'd got, together with the mail. 'The mail must go through!' was one of the precepts of the airline business in those days, so obviously we saved as much salvaged mail as we could get and we checked out all the papers and loaded that (sic), with what hand luggage we could find, onto the two station wagons and then started off.

The way back

Although I remember it as 105 miles it took us five hours to do the journey. That's not excessive when you think of the type of tracks we were travelling on, and not knowing the area at all, so it was a jolly good trip. The return was a bit easier because at least we knew which way we were heading and where we were going. We were very heavily loaded of course, because we were jammed tight with passengers, eight in each station wagon, and then we had cabin luggage packed in as well as we could, plus the mail which was lashed on the tailboard and on the roof. So we were heavily loaded vehicles and we couldn't take any chances that we might break axles or even tip off the tracks.

There was one woman who was sitting on the window side of the front seat (there was another fellow in between me and the passenger) and she would talk! She was an American woman; I discovered she was with her husband on her honeymoon and this was part of her honeymoon. Quite apart from hearing where she came from and what it was like, and what the wedding was like, what had happened at the wedding and the newspaper reports of the wedding, it went on and on and on. After a while, I suppose after the first hour or so, she was taking a breath and she said to me:

"I suppose you know why I'm talking?"

"Oh. yes."

And she said: "Well, why?"

"You're talking because you want to keep me awake; you're afraid I'll fall asleep."

She said, "oh, I didn't think you'd realise that, but you're quite right, I did want to see you didn't fall asleep because you've had a long day and it's a big strain driving through this country in the dark."

I said, "well, this is the thing you have to put up with," making light of it.

No sooner had I said that than I put the lights out and slammed the brakes on, and pulled to an emergency stop. There were a few screams and mutters around in the car and this American woman said, "well, what did you do that for?"

So I said, "didn't you see them?"

"See what?"

"There's a herd of buffaloes crossing the track in front of us and the last thing I want to do is get mixed up with buffaloes. Those are animals that scare me stiff."

She said, "only buffaloes?"

"Yes, they're only buffaloes, but quite honestly I believe they're the most dangerous animal there is in Africa."

She said, "oh dear, I didn't see them."

"Let's have a look now."

"Why did you put the lights out?"

"Because these animals at night time, they think of a light, if they don't smell it, it's not a fire, because it's a light they think therefore it's dangerous so they tend to charge on sight."

"Oh, oh," she says.

So anyway, I switched on the headlights and there was just the dust rising and leaves falling around where they'd crossed across the track, and so we carried on. It was funny though, after that it was very noticeable the conversation level was very much lower than it had been before, so obviously she must have realised that I was still awake, despite the fact that she had been worried about me!

Bare Essentials

We got into the Juba Hotel in the very early hours of the morning and the hotel manager organised things very well. He got the rooms sorted out, the places arranged, and the hotel servants rallied round so that people could get baths and so on. They went off to sleep for the rest of the night (well, there wasn't much left of the night) and I did my duty in the way of signalling what was going on, and advising headquarters for them to pass it on to London. Then I had the job of checking over the mail that I had got or hadn't got so I could report what was missing, and then I'm afraid I went and had a short sharp sleep too.

The next day I popped down to the only store there was in Juba and told them we had had this aeroplane problem and the passengers would need some odd things like razors or I don't know what they might want. Provided they were ordinary everyday items, not suits or anything (although they wouldn't have been able to get that there) they could charge it to the Airways account, to run a separate account, then I would clear that as all part of settling for the accident. So he was very happy, I was very happy, and as far as I could see, the passengers were very happy.

There was one little problem that arose and one of the female passengers came along to say they'd been down to the store to replace items that they wanted and it was all very nice and happy, but there was something they couldn't get. So I said, well what's all that about, and she said, well, it's, um, knickers, we can't get any replacements, they don't seem to have any ladies' knickers in that store, so we wondered if there's anything else that I could recommend.

Well, of course, this never struck me before, but I realised that all the European wives at the station, as they only did nine months and then went home on three months leave, they of course could equip themselves for the period of duty without having to bother to buy any extra clothes. They were just equipped when they came out to last up to a year. Then off they went back home again and re-equipped. I don't know what the wives of the Greeks did, or the Indians, but certainly, there were no facilities there for the English wives, and the black girls around there just didn't wear that sort of thing, they just had a little leather apron around their waist and that was it. The married women amongst them, they always had a skin slung over one shoulder and tied on the opposite shoulder, which indicated their status, but on the other hand covered very little.

Anyway, I wondered what might be the answer, so I went up to one of the government officials' wives and told her what the problem was. She said, "oh, that's all right, tell them to come up and see me." So I told the ladies, if they did have that problem to walk up the road to this house and ask for Mrs So-and-so and she would put them right. That seemed to be that and as I heard nothing after that, I assume the problem was solved.

After having had the passengers off that aircraft with us for about three days, we passed them on by the normal flying boat that came up twice a week. That sorted the passengers and the mail, but there was still the problem of the repairs, or whatever they were going to do about the aircraft. Although it was only 110 miles away from me, nevertheless it was in the 'other region', the Central Africa region, so technically it was out of my area, and Vernon Crudge, the manager of the Central Africa region, came across and got himself organised on the basis of 'it's my responsibility, I'll look after them'. However, he did use me as the place for communication, so that I occasionally got somebody coming in from that region with messages that they wanted this done or that done, or certain signals to be sent off. So I really became only the liaison officer for the Corsair business, even when the Short people came down and I arranged for them to get out to Faradge in order to get on with the repairs to the aircraft. I was only the middle man, I had no real responsibility.

The excellent Haynes Empire Flying Boat Owners' Workshop Manual *cites (p. 63) the Belgian Resident Officer driving the passengers to Aba where they were picked up by* Centurion. *They must have used the official report by Vernon Crudge. Geoffrey's anecdotes about the buffaloes and the underwear problem ring true.*

Chapter 12:
Life at Juba

Juba was different from Lindi. Although Lindi was the centre of a largish area and there was a district commissioner and a provincial commissioner, they seemed far less 'official' than the people in Sudan.

Juba was the headquarters of the Equatoria province and whilst in area it was considerably larger than Great Britain, the population density in the area was nowhere near that.

The Governor was responsible for everything that went on, and all of the staff there were directly responsible to him. The only people that weren't responsible to him, other than the two Indian traders and one Greek trader, were the padre and me in Airways. And as I fiddled around with the airport, initially the Governor was a little 'put out' and a little officious because he felt that he was going to have his authority and his connection with transport interfered with by these interlopers from Imperial Airways. But the incident of the landing on the airstrip when it was being refurbished, when they got round to asking my advice, meant I developed a working relationship with the Governor. I accepted him as the airport authority, nevertheless if anything went on in the airport other than maintenance it was expected that I would look after it. So I really worked along very happily under these arrangements.

Dress Code

Extra officialdom of the Sudan was especially noticeable in the dress code. The dinner dress was white trousers, white short-sleeved shirt, open neck with black cummerbund. Now this was expected of everybody for evening wear, even the government servants, be it public works or public health or those sort of people. Even in their own homes, they were expected to change into this 'informal' — although it Sudan it was the formal, dinner wear of the province. It was a thing that I felt was unnecessary, although when you get down to it, to have a discipline like this is one of the things that keeps you going in an area where there is very little, in the way of social codes and customs, to keep you on the straight and narrow. You could quite easily become so slack that you could almost become a castaway. You have to have certain disciplines that you carry out, and in the southern Sudan, you always changed for dinner. It was always the case that when you finished work you showered and changed, and you came and sat down, and had either drinks or a meal in the evening, having changed into this standard evening dress. Of course, the problem for us in the airways was that very frequently we didn't stop work at five o'clock. We rarely had time to shower or change before drinks or dinner, because if we were doing anything, we were working till eight, nine, ten o'clock at night, but it was expected that we followed the codes of the area. Mind you, we automatically wore long trousers or long sleeved shirts outside in the evening for our own protection, because the mosquitoes that come up just before sunset become very vicious. If you don't have long sleeves on to protect your wrists or arms, or long trousers so your knees and ankles are not bitten, you are very likely to go down with malaria.

My evening wear before was not shoes but what they called mosquito boots, and in point of fact they were the *stivali*, the uniform boots of the Blackshirts in Brindisi. While I was there, I realised that on the water, in the winter time, by wearing these boots of the Blackshirts, the *squadristi*, they kept your trousers, your legs, dry because the trouser leg got wet but you got your *stivali* up your trouser leg like a riding boot and it kept your leg dry and warm.

We Airways people had a limited amount of equipment, and what we had moved with us on transfer. I had kept my *stivali* with me, and I found them extremely useful as mosquito boots. So I didn't have to go investing in mosquito boots, I used these and, as they were black, with a black cummerbund and a white jacket it was good evening dress wear.

A tour of Juba, 1938

Juba itself was a very small area. There was a quay, where the river steamer tied up, and the wharf where they unloaded their stuff, not that there were enormous wharves there. Then there was the road running parallel to the river and the wharves which had two Indian stores on it, what they were I can't remember; then it came to the crossroads which was coming from the river straight up country running east to west, and that really was the main road of the town.

On the crossroads was the Greek bloke, Crassus; he was the one I used to deal with, practically anything that I wanted I went there. You went up from Crassus' store and you first came to the Juba Hotel. There was the crossroads just past the Juba Hotel and the left hand turn running south went down past the hospital down to the ferry. The one to the right went north to the aerodrome and the other side of the aerodrome was a track. It was just a track! I went up through it about four or five miles, and it just carried on through almost virgin country. It *was* virgin country in fact, and the most extraordinary animals you could run across there; anything from elephant, lion, buffalo, deer - all types of deer. I used to go out there solely to shoot guinea fowl, only because it made a change of diet. If I got a couple, I'd take them back and the chef would do his stuff in the kitchen, and then the radio man, the coxswain and myself had our special dinner of roast guinea fowl.

These birds are a small type of turkey, bigger than a chicken, but

I found them exceedingly difficult to shoot down, their feathers seemed almost like armour plating. I found the only real way to be able to bring them down was to fire at them when they were going away from you so that you got under the feathers, and you had to have some shot like SSG, anything less than that it seems to just bounce off them - extraordinarily tough birds!

Coming back to the main road, after you crossed the crossroads, the road carried on running west and on the right had side was the Mudeeria, that was the centre of government, the Mudeer was the Governor, and the place where he administered from was the Mudeeria. On the left hand side was a very good hospital; it covered Europeans and Asians and natives. There was a resident doctor in the town, and his wife was a senior nurse. There was one other British contract nurse and she had several native girls and fellows trained in nursing techniques. Anything I had to consult a doctor or hospital about, I was treated exceedingly well.

Carrying on, from then on up the road running west there were only the residences of the various offices of the administration: the district officer, the doctor's house, the nurse's house, the public works man, the public health man, the district officer, the agricultural officer and others. It was a complete town in itself, in the way of administration and people to administer, but the number of people in it, certainly white people, was 25 at the most.

Juba hotel and the Cairo to the Cape route

The hotel was quite a modern place. It was part of the Sudan Railways structure, because Sudan Railways ran the boat from Khartoum down to Juba. All down the river they had hotels so that if anything went wrong with the boats, the people could stay or stop there. There was one in Kosti and another in Malakal and there was this one in Juba. People didn't generally stay in the hotels but on board the boat. It was only when they got to Juba where the boat stopped that they were turned off the boat. They stayed in the hotel prior to going down by the railway cars, the station wagons; they went from Juba south to Laropi, on the Uganda border, which is past the rapids on the Nile, then on the still waters of the Albert Nile into Lake Albert.

Most people didn't realise that at that time there was a properly organised route for travellers all the way through from Cairo right the way down to South Africa. It wasn't by any means an extensive single route. Bits of it were by train, bits of it by truck, bits of it by ferryboat and then on by car and then by river steamer. The steamer went right the way down to Lake Victoria then on down by coach or car down to the Lake, Kivu, I think it was. Next there was a train service down through into Northern Rhodesia; and part of Northern Rhodesia again you went back into cars, then again train, then off and on trains all the way down to Cape Town. It really was a well organised, well co-ordinated means of transport all the way from the Cape to Cairo.

Coming back to Juba again though, what was it like living there? Well, the hotel was very good, well organised. It was run by a Greek manager, who had all his staff well organised and well trained, in fact, it was much better than living in your own mess and having to run it yourself and look after the staff. The main block was the restaurant with a bar and a number of toilets. Off the restaurant were the kitchens and laundry rooms, and on the other side of the restaurant was a big veranda. They used to put out sunshades and chairs so that you could sit on the veranda of the evening and have drinks and look out over the plains which looked north and north east, right across the plains which was an extraordinarily pleasant view.

Just outside the hotel, again on the northern side, they had two asphalt tennis courts and on one side of those, they had a swimming pool! All the white people in Juba swam whether it was during the day or the evening, whatever was convenient. I won't say that it was clean, it got very green before the water was changed, but at least it was a swimming pool. There were four showers alongside the pool, so you got out from a swim and you could wash off anything that might be clinging to you. Just alongside the swimming pool was a squash court. I didn't find anyone to play squash with me though! That worried me really, to find a squash court there like that and not a soul in the town would play squash!

Between the restaurant block and the sleeping quarters there was the road. It was a curved road coming off the main road to the hotel passing the sleeping block to get to the restaurant, and then sweeping round and out, so it was a U drive, really. Opposite the restaurant, across the road, was the sleeping block; they were double rooms, eight at the most, again well organised. You went through double mosquito doors onto a long veranda; the doors into each room led off that. Each end you had baths, showers, and toilets. At the back of the bedrooms, you had mosquito net all the way along, giving views out of the bedrooms over the entrance to the hotel to the bush country beyond. It was all mosquito proofed and it was very habitable.

Around the area there were also individual *"tuckles"* [a photo labels these TUKL] a single room with a thatched roof, doors, windows, et cetera. I rented two of these, one as an office for Imperial Airways – office accommodation, staff records, etc, and old typewriter we used for bashing out things. Another one was a rest room for staff. We were living in this hotel in single rooms; if you wanted to sit down and relax and put your feet up there was nowhere except the bar lounge in the main building. And we didn't want to sit in the bar the whole time when we'd got nothing on and we'd finished work and wanted to relax, so I rented one of these *tuckles* and got some furniture made by the local *fundi*, and equipped it so it was a restroom for us.

    I got in touch with the station superintendent down in Kampala, and asked him if he could somehow get hold of a lot of books cheaply, and then send them up to us, so I'd be able to have a reasonable sort of library that I and the other airways staff could read. Whenever any government officials were going home or retiring and selling up their property, he'd acquire some for me. He sent a jolly good set of books, they weren't all very expensive, but they were books, something we could all read, and I built up quite a library. Occasionally he used to send up more and sometimes I'd talk to passengers, not only Imperial Airways but also Sudan Railways passengers, who were fed up because they'd read all their books and there was nowhere to buy any new ones. I would let them have one of my books provided they gave me one to replace it. Sometimes they gave three books but only wanted another one, so I was able to build up quite a reasonable library there. It became quite popular not only with the railway blokes but also the government officials and their wives, because they found they ran out of reading material. Here was me with a library of assorted books and they only had to come down and put one in to take one out. We were all perfectly happy with it.

    Off the road from the entrance track to the hotel there was a long block, the equivalent of eight single rooms; it was the same as the other really, with the double mosquito net, the veranda and showers and toilets. That was one of the great things of Juba compared with my other postings at Mbeya, Lindi and Butiaba; here in the hotel we had running water on tap, water hot or cold, no problems with that, no problems with toilets either, we had flush toilets. It really was living in the lap of luxury compared with the places I had previously been!

    The single rooms were very plain, ordinary rooms, you went through the door and at the other end there was a window, can't call it a window really, an opening with mosquito net, and a washbasin and a bed, a chest of drawers and one chair. That was the standard night stop accommodation for a single passenger travelling with Sudan Railways. Of course we were living there permanently. There were only the three of us, but it really wasn't that restrictive, it was reasonable to live in by yourself if you just wanted to be quiet. If you wanted to you could go over to the lounge bar or of course in the case of the Airways staff, you could go over to the *tuckle* that I had equipped as a reasonable lounge with easy chairs, the library and a decent reading light. We could entertain our friends there; occasionally we invited people from the town, fellows and their wives, to take dinner at the hotel, then after dinner, we'd go across to our *tuckle* and have a liqueur or have coffee sent over to us and sit down and chat. I think there was a radio in the hotel lounge but I don't remember having a private radio in there at all. There was always the problem of batteries; in those days you hadn't got the modern equivalent and not only did you have to have an ordinary car battery but also an HT battery and if you ran out of that, well, you couldn't get them at all, you just had to wait until you got them from UK.

On the whole, because of the convenience of the hotel and everything like that, Juba was a much easier station to live than had been the others. The question of protocol irritated us. You had to remember the Governor was the boss of the district, and all the other civil servants, that is, all the other white people there, were responsible to the Governor. I'm afraid we Airways people took the mickey out of them rather. Because of the way they referred to the Governor, we started nodding our heads every time the word 'governor' was mentioned; after that we almost stood, we raised out bottom off the chair at the same time as nodding, almost bowing down! It became quite amusing really, the blokes that lived there, responsible to the Governor, they all saw the fun in it, and sometimes I think they deliberately mentioned the governor like that in order to see our automatic reaction to it. Of course, they did try it on when the Governor was present, but we didn't react on those occasions!

The swimming pool was the main recreation for many of us and the folks in the village. There were always quite a lot of people swimming, usually in the latish afternoon - about half past three to about half past four - that was your usual swimming time unless somebody was throwing a swimming party. In that case, it was usually drinks and a swim. I remember there were only about two or three of the wives that swam, so that it wasn't very prominent mixed swimming, nearly always males. On one occasion, I was in the swimming pool with about half a dozen fellows, and we hadn't bothered to put our swimming trunks on because there were just the males around. Suddenly one of the wives came along; she went into the hut, got rid of her dress, came out in her one-piece swimsuit, and dived in. The lads were terribly embarrassed; they were all swimming around and in came this one woman, the wife of the PWD man. I think she wondered why the boys kept away from her and didn't go over to talk to her. Well, we talked across the pool, but no close proximity. I often wonder whether she realised what was going on.

Church in Juba

I discovered very early in my stop at Juba that there was a catholic church there, only five minutes away from the hotel. It was just a mud hut with a grass thatched roof (makuti roof). I remember going along the first Sunday morning that I was there, walking up to the door in the end of the church as one normally expected, and I stood at the end of it and looked at the church; it wasn't terribly big I suppose about 25 yards long. It was filling up with crowds of the local natives, and one of the boys came down in a cassock; he'd obviously been sent by the priest. He said in the local dialect, which I didn't really understand, "Father said come with me." He took me out of the door I'd come through, around the left hand side of the church to a little door there. He opened the door and pushed me through, and I found that there was one kneeler with space for four, and a bench to sit on, and it was right on the side of the altar. I realised then that the priest had sent the lad around to put me in this chapel, if you like, so that I didn't mix with all of the locals, because it really was a crowd with lots of kids around. They all stood, no benches or anything, but I thought it was very decent of him, sorting me out and putting me on the side chapel, although it was only really a bench on the side of the sanctuary.

I was never able or, really, I never tried, to meet any of the priests because I found it difficult to communicate. Their native dialect was Mbgala, and although I got on workwise between Mbgala and Swahili, when it comes to conversation that would be a terribly difficult thing. The priests, I don't know what they were, I think most of them came from the Belgian Congo or something like that. I always remember on one occasion going to confession. The priest was sitting on the sanctuary, you knelt beside the priest and he heard your confession, and you had to get along between yourselves in whatever language you could communicate. I had Swahili, I had some French, I had some Italian, I had some Latin, but between us, kicking around between all the various languages we got through the sacrament perfectly happily. But we had confessions before mass, and kneeling up there on the altar trying to muddle through, with the rest of the people in the church standing down there, and being the only white person in the church, it could be quite embarrassing.

In retrospect I realise I really didn't make any effort to find out about the priests there, I was back into the church and I was happy at that. I regret that I didn't find out about the priests, what order they were or anything about them, because it could have made a lot of difference to me. On the other hand, after no churches at all in Mbeya, no churches at all in Lindi, to find you've got at least a mass going on each Sunday if not some days of the week as well, it really was a great relief.

There didn't seem to be much religion amongst the other white people there, they were all Church of England, Anglican. There was a padre there, he was a church missionary fellow, and I got on with him very well. Funnily enough, we never talked about religion and I didn't identify myself as being a Catholic. In those days, you didn't mention what your religion was. It became quite a habit with me to play chess with him. Occasionally he used to invite me over to his place for dinner and then we'd play chess; other times I'd invite him over for a meal in the hotel and then we'd go back to the *tuckle* and I'd set up my board there. It was a change from the usual routine.

Chapter 13:
Early 1939

At this time we had quite a lot of time on our hands, but amongst other things we used to go out in the car to look around the countryside. If we went out we always took extra water, extra petrol, a mosquito net, a gun and a spade, just in case, but occasionally also we crossed over the ferry and went up the east side of the river and went up to the emergency alighting area which was created up at a place called Mongalla. We went up there and we made this emergency mooring, and we occasionally used to go up there just to check that the emergency mooring buoy was still afloat, and clear away any weed coming down the river; the buoys might have clogged with the rubbish, which would have built up into floating platform, called sud.

Occasionally there was a wandering aeroplane came through. Sometimes there were intrepid birdmen flying and we'd get a signal saying they were due to come in. On those occasions it was my job to look out for them and see that the usual drills were carried out. They would be refuelled, we'd give them met. forecasts and met. reports for stations they were going to, we'd report to wherever they came from about them landing and send notices to those they were going to about when they were leaving. To me, of course, it was just ordinary handling routine, but it kept me interested. That is where I had brushes occasionally with the governor because he was always trying to point out that transport systems were under his authority but we got on all right together on the whole.

A couple of fellows that came through quite often were gold miners. They had the prospecting licence throughout Equatoria province and they wandered around seeing where they thought gold might be. They used to do a lot of washing in streams and picking around with picks to see what they could find. One was a Scotsman and the other was an Englishman; the Englishman was quieter but nevertheless still amusing, he was the senior of the two partners, and the other one was Parkey-Forbes. I never knew his Christian name he was just Parkey-Forbes to me. Mostly I met him in connection with alluvial, I mean washing, therefore gold, and they used to occasionally send a sealed cigarette tin up to Khartoum, presumably for selling or assaying. They sent a 50 tin of Players cigarettes, which were *the* way of buying cigarettes then, and having smoked the cigarettes they used to use the tins for the alluvial gold. They sealed it up with solder and wrapped it up to hide it, and they were delighted when I said I'd be prepared to take it up for them. I got my first lot of paid freight out of Juba from these lads with their alluvial gold. The great thing from their point of view was of course confidentiality. And because we as airline people were fairly well drilled in the security of valuable cargo we used to see that the information about their despatches didn't get out. They appreciated that and continued to send these little tins of stuff, which were declared as metal, of course, by our flying boats once the service started.

Of course these were the happy days of early 1939 when down in Juba we had these two flying boats northbound and two flying boats southbound each week. One of them was a through one between UK and Durban and the other one was down to Kisumu only. The northbound was one from Kisumu and one up from Durban. The only occasional visits we had from other aeroplanes apart from the casuals were from Sabena, who were operating in the Congo.

We tried to build up Juba, the flying boat station, and we got approval by the Governor and the Sudan Government and PWD for the erection of an "airport terminal" at Rejaf. The plans only showed that it was a through room with a bench across it. That was our passenger lounge with a customs bench and room for a customs officer behind it. The fact that the doors went right through the building, front and back for air, didn't matter; technically it was the passenger lounge and customs examination facility. Then on one side of it there was the store, in which we could keep not only our marine stores but also the standard spares for the engineering side and on the other side there was the office, and the "ablutions". They consisted only of three toilets: they were the 'long drops' which was a hole in a board over the top of a hole dug in the ground. There was a bench with water and a basin on it - that was the ablutions.

It was wooden structure, with a corrugated iron roof, but technically the layout covered all the requirements of an airport building. It was very much more comfortable and convenient after that, instead of having to stand under the shelter of the straw roof on the bank of the river and the radio operator having to work in the passenger launch all the time. So, then, we really felt we'd come and put ourselves on the map. We even had the PWD people paint on the roof the word J-U-B-A in great big capitals on top of this green roof.

But you know, this was all up to date, there was even one room for our radio station where we had our radio operator. He was on duty to pass weather conditions and also the usual routine messages in connection with the operation of the aircraft. If we had any messages that had to be passed up to ground stations, like up to Khartoum or down to Kampala, we broadcast them up to Juba station, which was a government controlled station, and they repeated the message to wherever it was supposed to go. We only had free access in radio to and from the aircraft.

Khartoum

In April 1939, Geoffrey handed over at Juba to Robbie Trench-Thompson, whom he subsequently worked with in Cairo.
At this stage he was transferred from Juba up to Khartoum. He had been in the 'unhealthy' stations in Africa, and had to complete his period of duty in Khartoum, which was not exactly a 'healthy' station, but at least not one of the 'unhealthy' ones. Health issues were the risk of malaria and all the other diseases in the tropical areas.
He lived in the Airways mess, a building requisitioned many years earlier, because Imperial Airways was long-established in Khartoum. It became quite an important place as a link station with the West Africa service.

The only thing I really remember about the time I spent in Khartoum was getting membership of the Sudan Club, which was one for the 'senior personnel' in the government. They called us 'senior personnel' and allowed us to become members. The great advantage of that was that they had a very nice swimming pool, and we used to take every advantage we could of using their swimming pool. I must admit I didn't use their tennis courts, but I did occasionally have a game of squash.

In later years, talking to people about life in Khartoum, I found mentioning that I was a member of the Sudan Club put me almost in the 'snob' bracket. I didn't know why because it wasn't that snobbish. Still, Khartoum was very much more protocol conscious than down in Juba. The Governor General lived there and had been established there for many years. As a transferee into Khartoum, I had a duty, following normal protocol, of calling on the Governor. As I was single, I only dropped cards on the Governor, one for him and one for his wife. It became very complicated if you were a married man and you visited either a bachelor governor or senior officer or a married senior officer; there was a very complicated code of dropping cards, I never really got round to understanding it. It was a silly thing really, when you realise that when you went into Khartoum of all places you had to see that you had properly engraved cards, because if you had printed cards you were really looked down upon: it had to be an *engraved* card. As I say the snobbishness was rife, I suppose it really was understandable because it was the senior station, with a long history, but on the other hand, it was a matter of discipline to be able to maintain standards under somewhat adverse conditions because, boy, was that station hot!

Khartoum was the hottest station other than Wadi Saidna, which was just outside Khartoum, which I didn't meet till several years afterwards; that was the hottest station that I ever worked in. But the great advantage was that it was dry: the humidity was extremely low. Provided you didn't pick up things that had been sitting out in the sun, and you didn't sit out in the sun uncovered yourself, you could tolerate the heat. There was fortunately a piped water system in the town - it was bucket sewage, but it was a well-organised city. It had a number of hotels, the best was the Sudan Hotel which was built on the Southern bank of the Blue Nile, that's the one that comes down from Ethiopia, as opposed to the White Nile, branching at Omdurman which comes down from Lake Victoria.

In May of 1939 Geoffrey got notice to report back to UK, having completed his three year tour; it had only been two and a half years, but being in the Central Africa area, the unhealthy area, the tour was reduced. He was flown up to Alexandria and from Alexandria through Brindisi, and via Rome, Marseille, and Bordeaux up to Southampton. He got home on 21st June, reported in and was sent on three months leave.

Chapter 14:
The Summer of 1939

Geoffrey came back to stay with his parents at Brogdale Road, Faversham for the duration of his leave. It was a vast change from the countries he'd been in for the last two and a half years. His first priority was to find some transport so he could get around and relax with old friends, visit old haunts. He was 24, and looking forward to enjoying himself, with company, social life and no mosquitoes to speak of.

I dashed down to Tankerton very early in my time there to investigate the possibility of getting a car. Then I realised I would have to get a licence first, because although I had an international licence, a Sudan licence, and a Kenya licence, the British licences authority wouldn't let me have one. I had to make an application and go to Maidstone and plead my case to be allowed a visitor's licence for three months. That meant I could successfully negotiate for a car, which I did by going down to the big garage at Tankerton, Pratts, I think it was. I had a long chat with a fellow that I knew from my earlier days around. I didn't really mind what it looked like, as long as it was sound mechanically, I just wanted it to get me around well, while I was on holiday, and after the three months I would be selling it. The fellow said he had just what I wanted. He turned out a Ford A Model, a 14.9 hp job, four cylinders it was, but it was a real 'standy-up' type of car. But I successfully drove it around for the three months that I was on holiday and thoroughly enjoyed it. It went like a bomb, it would go anywhere, climb any hill, go through mud, go through dirt and bush, it was a lovely vehicle. I had no trouble at all with it, I used to just put petrol in it and go.

I picked up quickly with the gang from Tankerton. One day when I went down to join them they said they were going over to Canterbury to see the new film which just arrived, the great rage, and they said would I like to come? So I went along to see *The*

Four Feathers, which includes a battle at Omdurman, just outside Khartoum. It looked very terrible and everybody suffered around that area; it looked so terrible that, because they knew I had been for a time around Khartoum, my shares absolutely soared. I became one of the most famous people that had been in darkest Africa!

I called, of course, back up at Ravenscourt, to see my old schoolmaster, Mr Hutchinson. We were always great friends; anyway, I went up there and had a chat with him. He invited me to stay for tea and meet some of the family again. I heard the news about the family, and subsequently on a visit, one of the older girls, Mabel, said she and her fiancé David and some other people were going camping, and would I like to come along? I was only too delighted! They were particularly keen to have me with them because it meant they had another car available.

The only thing I remember about the camp now was being asked if I would go down to Faversham to pick up Mollie, one of Mabel's younger sisters, who was joining the crowd at the camp. As I was a spare man with a spare car, I thought, that's no trouble at all and I went down to pick her up. When I met her again, I realised she was not the little schoolgirl that I used to know, she was much more mature; in fact, she was working as a nurse in London, the Middlesex Hospital. I said to myself, there's something about this girl. When we were in the camp, I enjoyed her company and I think she enjoyed mine, and we had a jolly good holiday. The camping was in August, which was the middle of my three months because I'd got July, August and September free. We wandered round the countryside, and did things, and thoroughly enjoyed ourselves. Then, of course, we heard by listening to the radio the possibility of war being declared and we decided that we'd better pack up camp. Several reasons: of course I didn't know what was going to happen and thought I might be posted to Germany immediately if war was declared; Mollie thought she would be called back to the hospital, and David was an auxiliary fire service man and he thought he might be called. The others also had various commitments, so we decided we'd pack up camp and we went our various ways.

   I got in touch with my headquarters to find out what they wanted me to do. They just confirmed my address, and told me to stay and carry on for the period of my leave. They gave me a contact number, which was in Bristol because they were evacuating the Head Office there from London.

The rest of my leave was really rather depressed because of the declaration of war. I hadn't anything to do because I was on holiday, so I went down to the local civil defence people and offered my services.
"Well," they said, "you'll only be with us a short time, is it worth it?"
"Ok, so I'll help you out for the short time that I'm with you."
They thought a bit and said, "we were thinking of doing a test tomorrow, would you like to do emergency ambulance driving, you've got a car."
"Oh, sure, sure."
"Do you want a pilot, because you've only just come and you have to know the roads, and all the short cuts, and where things are and so on."
So I had to point out to them that I had been born and brought up in the area and I'd gone to the Grammar school and it was only because I worked overseas that I was considered to be a visitor to the place.
That settled it down and a couple of evenings later I operated as an emergency ambulance in my little car. We called her Miranda. I don't know who got the name, or where we got it from or how, but anyway, my Ford was called Miranda. I used it for the emergency ambulance for the exercise and got around well with no trouble at all.

The emergency headquarters for civil defence seemed to me a sort of oddity; they hadn't thought it through properly. One night I was sitting there in the central control purely waiting for something to happen, and somebody came down and we got talking. The fellow seemed to be a regular and talking things over I made comments about certain things I was supposed to do and that were supposed to happen if there was an emergency of one type or another. I made suggestions as to what could be improved, and I thoroughly took it to pieces and said what I thought ought to be done in order to be able to reorganise the headquarters of our local civil defence. About three months later after I'd gone back to work, I came to visit my parents for a quick weekend. I found that in the civil defence they had taken up practically all of the recommendations and suggestions. The fellow I'd been talking to on that evening was in fact the fellow responsible for the town's civil defence! So I had made my points to the right people, quite by accident.

At the end of September, my leave was up, so I got in touch with my people who were then in Bristol. I was told to report down to Bristol and check in, so I said my goodbyes to home and to parents, and off I went down to Bristol to find out what was doing.

PART TWO:

Love and War

Chapter 15:
Imperial Airways HQ on evacuation

The war changed the face of British civil aviation. The European services were cancelled, since the many of the countries became enemy territory. There was political argument about the role of independent companies, and Imperial Airways merged into British Overseas Airways, then after the war into BOAC and BEA. Emotionally the employees still worked for the organisation that was family, where the customer always came first. So, we enter Geoffrey's war years.

In Bristol, Imperial Airways were still pretty disorganised and not quite catching up with what the war was doing to them. They were still operating services, but with the impossibility of air activity over anywhere between England and Germany, they were having to send our flying boats around the coast of France to keep away from German aircraft. France was in the war too, but the 'boats operated down to Bordeaux then from Bordeaux across to Marseille. Subsequently they also did a call down to Lisbon. The services continued through to Bordeaux and Marseille on to the Mediterranean and then out to India and Burma, and down to South Africa.

But as the war progressed into what was named the phoney war it was obvious that all the European operations that Imperial Airways had been doing, which of course had been immediately cancelled, could in fact be helpful. Certain of those operations could be reinstated. As a result, they reopened Croydon because there was no bombing and the flying boats operated out of Southampton, anyway. So the 'powers that be' decided to reopen the terminal up in London, which was a lovely big building that had only been opened in 1938.

Airways House really was a magnificent place. It was reopened as a terminal point for the operations into Europe, down to South Africa, and for the Far East. Fortunately, I was asked to go up and start these European operations from Victoria. I wondered what I was going to do for accommodation; I stuck a notice on the common room notice board saying I was going up to Victoria and if anybody had any accommodation they'd had to leave to come to Bristol, could I rent it until I went overseas again. I was very lucky and several people rang me up. One particular lass rung me up and she had got a mews flat in West London on a long lease and she was only too delighted to let me have it and everything in it; it was a completely equipped. I settled in there and she not only gave me the telephone number of the woman that used to 'do' for her, but phoned up the woman herself to tell her that she had let the flat to me, it was all above board. It was very comfortable, very useful. It was only a short walk down to the Underground then I went straight on the line to Victoria. Then I walked down Buckingham Palace Road to the new terminal, which as I say was a beautiful place, opened less than a year earlier.

I always remember the fellow in charge of the building, the General Services Superintendent, a fellow called Henderson, very nice, a charming fellow, very efficient; he was wandering about the building when I first went there to find out what it was all about. He let me in and showed me around, and we had a chat. and he said, "of course the *pièce de resistance* of this new building is the ladies toilets, they are absolutely marvellous." And I said, "well the building's empty, let's go and have a look at them!" So we went down and they really were absolutely magnificent, I don't know, they were like individual boudoirs, absolutely fantastic — I'd never seen any toilet blocks like that before in my life! They really were something worth writing home about.

I had three or four staff posted to me and we started these operations into one or two European points, I forget now what they were. But of course they were all operated by dark. I presume now it was the blackout in case of air raids, but it meant we had to work by lamplight, checking in passengers and checking passports and all our administration. We settled into a routine, even though it was in the dark, and I was able to do some useful work up there. In Bristol, I was just duty officer which meant answering the phone when nobody else was there and passing the message to the person that was due to receive it. It was really quite a bore, being duty officer on a routine basis like that.

It came in very useful, being at Victoria and at the mews flat there, as, having met Mollie camping, and having been rather taken with her, we met several times when neither of us were working. Her real name was Frances, and I started calling her that, and never really returned to calling her Mollie. We were able to spend time together, and it ripened into more than we thought it ever would. I think both of us decided that things were serious between us and we looked forward to the possibility of getting married. But on the other hand we were very worried because I didn't know what was going to happen to me in the next two or three months, where I was going or what, so we were sort of unofficially engaged, but hesitant of what was going to happen, with the war having just started.

However my posting came through with about three or four days notice, and I had to pack and leave, as I was posted to Alexandria as one of the station officers.

Chapter 16:
Alexandria and Cairo

Although Geoffrey still has fascinating stories about his activities and relationships through the war, he says little about the actual operations, especially in Cairo, the hub of the Horseshoe route. The habit of secrecy filtered through to his memoirs – or maybe it was just that day to day operations were too routine to remember. Details that might be fascinating to historians were of no worth to him. An example of this is one piece of paper he used for notes when he was sorting out his archive: it was the back of a loading sheet for one of the 'boats - two a penny to him, but a historical document now. Equally, he stopped taking photographs. Maybe the incident with the 'traveller' and the mine layer in Brindisi was part of this. Maybe he was just too busy.

At that time, late 1939, Alexandria was the centre of the Near East Division. This covered the area along the African coast down to the Southern Sudan border and out to Iraq, and then on down the Persian Gulf to include the Gulf States, but it didn't include Beluchistan, the other side of the water, which came under the Indian Division. At Alexandria, I settled into a pension called the Reinerheim, which was very a nice little pension, run by Austrians. There were between six and ten of us resident there. It was on the Corniche between the two hotels that were used by Imperial Airways, one of which was the Cecil. It was convenient for contact with the passengers that were in Alexandria, and it meant that the transport run by the company could easily pick me up and take me down to the airport. This was the flying boat base at Ras El Tin. The base there had its offices on the quay, but the offices were almost tarred boxes. They had been made out of the crates containing the aircraft bodies and wings exported to Egypt over a period of several years. When the aircraft bits had been taken out of them, these boxes were just settled down and holes made here and bits stacked on there, not only to make a set of offices, but also the passenger waiting room and the customs examination section too. Ras El Tin had been our flying boat base for a very long time, because of the Calcutta flying boats that operated for years between Brindisi, Athens and Alexandria, and the Kent class, which was the four engine one before that.

Of course there was a lot of uncertainty in Alexandria and the Near East area, because of the war. Germany had a lot of influence in various areas in the Middle East and we didn't know whether they were going to cause upset in Iraq or Iran (which was still Persia). If they did then it could cut our operations. So the local governors didn't quite know what to do, what to plan, because they didn't know how the war was going to develop. At this time it was almost a stalemate in Europe, still this period of the phoney war.

A little semaphore

There was an incident in 1940 that formed the start of my tie-up with the RAF. I was on duty, waiting for one of our 'boats to come in, and there was an RAF float plane wandering around by our part of the harbour - around and around, and backing up and down. There was someone in the cockpit waving his arms like mad, and I recognised he was semaphoring, so I said to my coxswain "What is he saying?"

He said he wouldn't know, so I said "Wait a minute, you're supposed to be trained in semaphore" (the requirements were for Morse and semaphore for coxswain), and he said "Well, I've never had anything to do with that."

This fellow was still waving his arms around, so I put my hands up in a signal I remembered from when I was a Boy Scout, or even a Cub, indicating that I was conscious he was trying to do something, and he started off again but his arms were waving around like crazy. So I tried to spell out s-l-o-w-e-r but I couldn't remember what w was, so I spelled s-l-o-e-r and the fellow on the plane acknowledged that and he started waving his hands again but he did it very slowly and I was able to read what he was saying and it was simple!

"Please can I use one of your moorings."

And we hadn't got any! So I grabbed the coxswain and told him to get on the launch and take him up to buoy number whatever it was. Subsequently the pilot of that plane and his observer came ashore and we had a chat about none of us knowing how to communicate. Anyway he was grateful.

Subsequently he went to the RAF Mess which was established in what had been previously the Yacht Club in Ras El Tin, and he invited me along to meet the fellow in charge there and have a chat to them. As a result, I found out that they anticipated receiving a Solent squadron from the Far East coming up for operation in the Mediterranean. The Solent was the military craft developed from our C Class flying boats; we had long chats and he used to ask me all sorts of questions. Over time, we established a relationship which I found very helpful and he obviously did too. I'd received a communication from my boss, Maxwell, who was Middle East Regional Manager, that I would be moving in a very short time to take over Sharjah in the Gulf. This would have been quite an interesting posting because at that time Sharjah was really just a *Beau Geste* type of fort which was built around a well; we had our own armed guards, almost a little army that patrolled day and night, we had gates that were locked, it really was a fortress, because there were only marauding tribes around, no civilisation, only marauding tribes fighting against each other. But we had to keep ourselves well protected or else they'd come in and pinch everything we'd got. We had to protect our airstrip too. At that time we had land planes going eastbound as well as flying boats, so I thought I'd be posted there, it wouldn't be too bad, and though it was 1940 it didn't worry me too much. But I suddenly heard that the posting had been cancelled and I'd be remaining in Alexandria.

I later found out that it was because of the RAF indicating to their Air Commanding in Alexandria that they didn't want me to move away because I was so helpful to them at Ras El Tin; they didn't want to lose me. So fortunately, Maxwell then accepted what the AOC RAF wanted and stopped my posting, which was very useful!

Marriage progress

During this period, I was corresponding with Mollie, or rather, Frances, and we confirmed that we wanted to get married. I was planning to get her out to Alexandria so we could get married the following June or July, 1940.

I had many formalities to go through before that. I applied to my boss who was the Traffic Director at Head Office, because I was still a Traffic Operator, for permission to get married. This was one of the things you had to do, you had to get permission to be married; I gave the details of Frances, applied to him to get permission, and I also wrote to her parents because I'd never spoken to her mother or father about the possibility of getting married! I wrote telling them what I intended and what my prospects were in the airline business. I also let my mother know because obviously she would also be a very interested party.

At the same time, I was looking into the possibility of a flat around the Alexandria area, so that we could get married and move into our own accommodation. I was confident that if I got permission for marriage, I would be able to wangle a seat for her out of UK to Alexandria. I didn't check over any sort of church because I thought that would be going far too far ahead and I wanted to wait until we got together again before I did that sort of thing.

Work on the ground continued, of course. We were not really doing anything spectacular, the flying boats were coming out from England, across Italy and down, then going on either to South Africa or the Far East and we worked in our usual way of having a 24 hour period on duty and then 24 hours off. If we were unlucky, we would be working through for about 18-20 hours, but if we were normal we would get at least six hours sleep during that period of 24 hours work. It was really rather pleasant; if things didn't go wrong you had quite a long period where you could go out and enjoy yourself, either sailing, swimming, playing golf or going down to whatever club you belonged to and thoroughly enjoying life.

I got a reply to my official application to get married which was affirmative, saying 'yes, my marriage was approved and it would go on my record as being an approval' so that when I decided to get married then I wouldn't have any trouble. I also got a reply to my letters from both Mrs and Mr Hutchinson: Mr Hutchinson wrote rather on the basis of 'thank goodness - I've just heard that my wife is answering your letter, so I'll leave it to her', whereas Mrs Hutchinson did write a long letter, a welcoming letter, and one which I very much cherished.

Then came the problems.

The Horseshoe Route

In June 1940, Italy declared war and joined the Germans. They became known as the Axis. This meant our flying boats could not come across Italy and we had to find a way around without crossing Italy *and* not crossing Libya, because Libya and Tripolitania were then under the Italian flag. North Africa and Italy were closed to us.

Next, we had trouble with Abyssinia, because the Italians had been colonising in Abyssinia and Eritrea, and we were caught in the middle. With the stoppage of the flying boat connection between London and Alexandria, we really had to start thrashing ahead to find out how we could continue our operation; what would be the best thing to do for UK and towards the war effort to continue using our flying boats.

A decision was taken at headquarters and we then started what we called 'the Horseshoe route' which was flying boats coming up from South Africa to Middle East and from Middle East out to India and the Far East. This started with one or two flying boats because we hadn't got all of them overseas: some of them were caught in the UK, so we had a limited number of flying boats, and of course we had only our normal overseas base type of engineering. We hadn't got any major engineering because that had previously been done at Poole.

We then had the scare that Alexandria could possibly be raided, by the Italians or any supplementary fleet of the Germans that might get into the Mediterranean. At the time, we were definitely worried about the Italians, because not only could they start bombing Alexandria, but also their ships might get in and play havoc with the harbour and our operations there. On the 25th May 1940, Alistair Thomson, at that time station superintendent at Alexandria, was promoted to acting regional traffic superintendent to take the place of Bill Teague who was moved down to Durban in order to establish a sort of overseas headquarters for the Horseshoe route. As a result, I was promoted to Station Superintendent Alexandria. It didn't last very long. We evacuated Alexandria as a flying boat base, and the land plane base at El Nouzha, and moved all our operations down to Cairo on the 20th June 1940. We then used Cairo as the junction point for the South African and Far Eastern operations.

Cairo

So I went down to Cairo as the Station Superintendent. This meant I not only had responsibility for the flying boat operations in and out of Cairo - which used the bit of the river that was known as Rod El Farag - but also for the land plane operations out of Heliopolis.

In moving down I wasn't too certain about taking my car with me. Fortunately I found a fellow in transport in Alexandria, who was also in the transport business in Cairo; it was a family firm, I gather, a fellow called Hanafi. He offered to drive my Morris Minor down to Cairo for me, some time when his father was transferring stuff, so that if he broke down he'd have someone to back him up and he wouldn't get stuck in the hundred and fifty miles between Alexandria and Cairo. So I also had my Morris Minor out in Cairo, which became an extremely useful asset.

I took up accommodation in a pension, the Pension Elite. It sounds posh, but it wasn't! It was only an ordinary sort of pension, just about the same as the pension I was using in Alexandria, same type of building, the same service, very much the same. There were more people in the Elite and it was up on the fourth floor, and I shared a double room. I tried to insist on a single, but it made my costs lighter and it was more convenient to have somebody in the firm also living in the same accommodation. I shared the room with Robbie Trench-Thompson, who had taken over at Juba when I'd gone to Khartoum, but there were two other fellows in the same pension, Lawrence Young and also a fellow whose surname was Rice.

With the move of our operations to Cairo and closing down Alexandria, we also got what was called then a Regional Manager. Previously we had just a Manager, Middle East, but then we had this new bloke brought in and some slight reorganisation. He was a fellow that none of us knew, none of us had met him before, and we subsequently found that he was a senior type of person in Athens tramways. We used to call him Mr Tramways till we got to know him more about him. I don't think there was really anyone that liked him at all. It was pretty obvious from our point of view and from the Works point of view that he was in the Middle East to make a name for himself during the war and work towards getting himself a knighthood or something like that. He was out to look after himself by using us as much as possible in order to achieve his own objectives. He was always having meetings at the Middle East home joint services, why I don't know, but he made his name around the military circles and also as a member of the Turf Club; he really got himself well into the higher echelons of the war waiting machinery. Consequently, we were finding ourselves more and more tied and having to work increasingly in conjunction with the military.

Of course, working with the RAF had always been a thing with us. Any co-operation with the RAF we didn't mind at all, it always came as natural, but it did come a little bit rough when we had to start working in conjunction with the army and doing things which normally we wouldn't do under normal circumstances, but it pleased and it got kudos for Robert Maxwell.

Our head office was trying desperately to find a way to link up the UK with the rest of the Commonwealth. France was now occupied. Air runs up and down the coast of France, and flying boats that went up there, were subject to raids by fighter patrols. There was also a problem with the Spaniards, who seemed to be leaning towards the Axis as well. Portugal seemed to remain more or less neutral, and Lisbon seemed to be a point where we could get from UK to Lisbon then down to Gibraltar, but it was obvious that Lisbon was the centre of espionage both for the Allies and for the

Axis. Suspicions in Lisbon were certainly so great that you never spoke to anyone about anything seriously unless you were either in a room that you were absolutely sure was bug-proof or way out in the open where no-one could possibly trace you or put surveillance on you. Mind you, this didn't affect me, because I wasn't in that line, but I certainly heard many comments from people that you had to be terribly careful because you might be passing information of use to the enemy. It made life exceedingly difficult for head office trying to make a connection out to the Middle East again. With France under occupation, the French colonies were also anti-Ally, certainly not in any way neutral, consequently we couldn't use the French colonies down on the west coast of Africa to get to the nearest of the British colonies, Gambia and Sierra Leone.

There was still the operation from Khartoum across to West Africa, but the only aircraft we had operating on there was the De Havilland DH86. Although it was very useful and successful in the operation for which it had been developed, both for mail and passenger carrying, it was not the sort of thing that you could develop into a major operation.

At the end of 1940, I transferred from Station Superintendent Rod El Farag, responsible for the flying boat operations between South Africa and the Far East, and I went down to Juba once again. Actually I was happy going back down to Juba because I knew the station, and I knew the people, and it was a happy place. In Cairo at that time life was exceedingly difficult and we really had no relaxation. I spent a couple of months in Khartoum at the start of 1941, investigating the other options from there, before going to Juba in the March.

Chapter 17:
Return to Juba

Things built up in the beginning of 1941 down in Juba, because it became obvious that Imperial Airways, or rather British Overseas Airways, could link up at Juba with several operations, not only the land planes up from South Africa but also the developing Sabena operation in the Congo.

Sabena had already started to operate across from the Congo up to us in Juba. They used to bring up the loads they wanted to get onto our main line service either down to South Africa or up to the Middle East, or to the Far East for that matter, and we would pick them up on the flying boats. At the same time, for anyone going out to West Africa who wasn't able, or for whom it wasn't practical, to do Khartoum-Lagos on the little land plane, they came down to Juba and waited until there was some space on the Sabena operation. That went through the Belgian Congo from Juba down to Stanleyville, Stanleyville down to Leopoldville, Leopoldville up to Duala, and Duala up to Lagos. My French slowly acquired the necessary aviation words so that I could communicate reasonably well with the pilots and crew. The workload in Juba kept increasing as not only did we have two flying boats northbound and two flying boats southbound each week, but now we were getting the two planes a week coming in from the Congo and going out to the Congo, with passengers offloading at Juba to switch to the other service. It all made life more interesting as there was always something to do. Having people night stopping meant that we saw some people from the 'outer world'. Otherwise, most of us had just been stuck in Juba for months and months and only had information from around Juba or from the radio stations. Now we were meeting people that knew something of what was going on.

Some of the people I remember we had were the people from Yugoslavia. I can't remember whether they were Chechniks or what the other group were, but they were being evacuated from Albania and taken round to the UK in order to be able to get training and information, or so I assumed. Boy, were those tough cookies! They really were rough, tough people, and although we were able to get on with them, they didn't speak a word of English of course and you had to get along with them in either Italian or French, but they really were tough guys. They got very fed up when they were told after they'd landed that they'd got three days to wait before they were able to go off on one of the Sabena flights round through the Congo up to Lagos. Of course, when they got to Lagos they would then again have problems getting through to the UK.

Increasing workload

At this time, we had the development of the flying boat coming down via Lisbon round to Lagos. This helped tremendously not only because the flying boats had explored the route, but also Airways acquired a couple of Martin flying boats. I forget how many, but these flying boats came from the United States, I don't know whether it was lease-lend or whether they had to buy them, but it did mean we had these two flying boats up in the UK and, with their range, able to operate from the UK down to Lagos with a good commercial load.

1941 really was for us in Africa a real developing time, not only with the Sabena operation but also the South African forces were increasing up in the western desert. In order to keep communication with them from South Africa, the South African Air Force started a transport operation for their own people and for mail and communications, equipments generally, all the way through from Johannesburg to Cairo through Juba. When they first came through Juba, they were very pleased with the stop; it was a night stop they made there for the first proving flight. They found that we knew what to do, how to look after them. We could get all the weather [reports] organised, and the forecasts organised. They came in, and, having landed, stayed the night and gone on, they were only too happy that they'd found a well-organised station with whom they'd be able to work with no troubles.

The bookings on the regular flying boats, up and down from South Africa to Cairo, were fairly full, so we were getting backlogged with passengers in Juba wanting to join them from the west coast. They started a shuttle land plane service from Khartoum down to Juba, and it finished up that we were having more night stops at Juba in any week than Khartoum had at any time before. At that time there was only myself and the coxswain and the radio operator, so I sent an appeal for help and fortunately I was sent down a clerk. It was rather amusing, because I'd gone off one day down to the flying boat base at Rejaf, looking after the flying boats both north and south, but I knew there was a landplane coming into the aerodrome from Khartoum. All I could hope was that the routine that I'd established there with the hotel to pick up passengers and the Shell agent to refuel the aircraft would work out all right.

At Rejaf I had a phone call from Juba. On the other end was the fellow saying, "the land plane has arrived and I am Abdul Bahi, I've been sent down on transfer to Juba to join you as your station clerk. And I thought you'd like to know, I've sent off the arrival signal, and I've arranged for hotel accommodation for the passengers, and I've also booked with the Met Office that they get a forecast at [such and such a time] for tomorrow morning so the skipper ..." and on and on he went. He'd done all the routine and everything that was necessary and I could just sit back and say "Oh, that's a lucky break!"

I hadn't met Abdul Bahi before, but after he arrived, life became so much easier. He knew the routine, he knew the stuff and as he was an Arabic speaker, he didn't have to stutter with his Arabic like I had to. Not only that but he had been based in Juba when it was a landplane station in the earlier days, so he knew the station itself as well. He knew the hotel, he knew the aerodrome, in fact it was he that had put the Imperial Airways' equipment into a mud hut just off the edge of the aerodrome and put a padlock and key on it, for the time when we came back again. We had salvaged that equipment when we first got back there in 1938! He also knew, or was known by, the local government officials and the customs officials, so he was a great asset. He was also a very pleasant fellow.

Subsequently, in the 1960s I think, Abdul Bahi was then the General Manager of Sudan Airways, a position I'm sure he was more than qualified for (although I gather that in the 1970s he disappeared absolutely; basically it was political events that got him to disappear, but we never heard exactly what happened to him). A couple of times we invited Abdul Bahi to come along and join us at trainees' reunions, which he did, and he thoroughly enjoyed meeting us. I always remember when he was asked what was the toughest time he had when he was down in Juba, and he said, "Oh that was with Geoffrey Pett when we were building up the station to cope with the expansion of services up to the Middle East." That was a nice little pat on the back for me; I was very pleased! Particularly as it was among a group of Trainees who were men that had made their names in aviation generally.

Busy, busy at Juba

With the war effort continuing in the Middle East and the desert fighting, there was intense effort in order to be able to reinforce the Middle East consequently Juba became quite an important part of the air network.

During this year, still 1941, things really became hectic down in Juba, so many odd things happened and I can only remember the outstanding ones. Like the time we had so many planes coming in for night stopping - so many passengers and crews to be put up - that we got the married people sleeping along the married quarters of the hotel, and we got beds put up all the way along the verandah there. We got another lot of beds put up on the verandah of the single quarters, so that was full up, and I even had to call on the hospital, to let us have some extra beds. We even used corridors in the hospital in order to be able to accommodate some more of them. By the time you'd got hospital beds made available in the hotel, corridors in the hospital made available, the corridors in the married quarters of the hotel and the single quarters of the hotel, and the TUKLs doubled up as well, it really was quite a lot of fun handling these services. The chef of the poor hotel had never been so busy in his life! It worked all very well, and we found that people took the rough with the smooth, because after all, it was wartime and most people accepted that there was an emergency on.

It was noticeable that the nicest people to deal with were the very senior officers, particularly the naval officers, I found. The senior naval officers were very nice types. The RAF senior officers were all well and good, we spoke the same language. The army officers, well, they were a little different. They seemed to be so totally different from the navy and air force senior officers. When I say 'senior officers' generally I mean anyone above major. Majors were the worst, Colonels and Majors – they were shockers!

Every time we had trouble with some military passenger, it was always a colonel. The trouble with them was always 'oh, well I'm not going to stay here four days for that flight, I've got to go on, I'm priority, you see!' and so they used to moan like mad. Previously, if passengers came down and they had some priority, I would already have a signal from the Middle East Headquarters indicating who was to travel on what aircraft out and what the priorities were. So when these people came along and complained they had to stay three days in Juba before they could get away on a plane via the Congo to Lagos, they'd carry on about being priority.

I'd say, "Sorry, I can't do anything."

"Well, I'm going to do something."

"What do you want to do?"

"I'm going to get in touch with the priority authorities!"

"All right, well, you'll have to go down to the telegraph office, and the telegraph office is down there and this is the address of the Headquarters Middle East and this is the person you want to get in touch with, and you can, you'd better get in touch with them and we'll see what happens."

Well, this worked time and time again, but one fellow, a senior man heard me telling this one particular bloke about this and afterwards he said to me:

"It's extraordinary, you know. Why do you give him the option to be able to go down to the telegraph station? And even the address of the priorities board?"

"Well, I know jolly well that by the time he sends his signal off, it won't get up to the Middle East to be handled till after the plane's gone tomorrow morning, so even if the reply were to come back to say, 'yes you can go on the next plane', it will have already gone. But," I said, "in any case it doesn't really matter, because it makes him happy. I don't worry because it takes him off my back, because I know darn well that when the reply comes back he'll do as he's told; the priority's laid down and that's it, we're not changing the priority."

It was just a way of getting him off my back and knowing jolly well that he wouldn't change anything anyway. But apart from that we went along and we had quite easy going – we got so used to the problems arising that we just took them in our stride.

One of the blokes working in the Sudan Government service in Juba came back from some leave one time having got himself married! This was rather nice for him, and I joined the party to welcome his wife to Juba and found that it was a girl that I knew who worked for Imperial Airways up in Cairo. So this was marvellous, I knew this girl from Cairo, and I knew her work. But I also knew that although Bahi used to do some of the typing and stuff, and he used to do all he could, but he didn't take shorthand or anything like that, and between us, me tapping the typewriter, him tapping the typewriter, it really overloaded what spare time we had. So I spoke to her about whether she could do some work for us, and she said she'd be delighted!

To get this arranged, I sent a signal to Headquarters saying I needed a clerical staff and I'd got one and who she was, and I proposed to take her on. Fortunately, the signal went to the man that she used to work for in Cairo; he recommended that I employ her and give her status and recommended pay level too. She was delighted because it meant she was keeping in touch with what she'd been doing in Cairo, at the same time it gave her some pocket money and it gave her something to do! In Juba there was very little for the wives to do. She'd got her servants to look after the house, all she could do then was chat to the few other wives that were left there, or play tennis, or go to the hotel swimming pool and swim there. You couldn't go for a walk, because it was much too rough to be able to go walking in. So she was delighted to have this 'spare time occupation' but it relieved both Abdul Bahi and myself from a lot of the clerical work and the reports! There were so many reports! Running a station meant there were reports for every aspect of operation, and then there were the routine summaries to be completed, these every month and others every week, and she was able to do all that, just on information I would leave in the office. She came in, saw the notes, and did what was necessary; it made an enormous amount of difference!

Night landing

It was at this time when the radio station attached to the Sudan Communications Centre got a call from an aeroplane on its way to Juba and they indicated they would be arriving after or just around the period of dark. They knew there were no facilities for night landing at Juba. Because it was received by the government radio, this information was immediately passed up to the provincial governor because he was theoretically the boss of all the areas. The governor, Martin Parr, didn't know what to do: he couldn't very well signal back 'you mustn't come to Juba you'd better go home', because where would the poor fellow get to? Fortunately, he rang me and I was able to ascertain what the ETA was likely to be. From my point of view it was quite an easy point. But it was interesting because Martin Parr had, a little while earlier, made it quite clear to me that he was the boss of everything attached to the airport. As the governor of the province he was responsible for all military as well as all civilian matters and this business of Imperial Airways doing things on the aerodrome without his knowledge was contrary to responsibilities. So when he had to ask me to look after this aeroplane that he had nothing whatsoever to do with, it reinforced the authority that the Station Superintendent of Imperial Airways had over movement of aircraft. It was a silly little thing, but under local circumstances and in relation with the government and the civilian people like myself it really made a major difference.

I had no trouble of course because all I had to do was to call my local boys, the boat boys I used down at Rejaf. I got them rounded up and we got hold of half a dozen empty petrol tins, the four-gallon drums that I could easily get from Shell agent, stuffed them full of grass, and put them down the runway and across the runway, the usual L configuration. At the same time I called the local government officials, all eight I think, if they would come up with their cars or trucks or whatever they had to the airport at a certain time, because we had this aircraft landing after dark.

This was great excitement for them! We got them, and I put them on either side of the runway in a herringbone system, so the lights wouldn't shine into the aircraft as it was landing – you know this was the sort of thing you would naturally do, just from dealing with planes and things. I told everybody, the boys with the petrol cans and the drivers of the cars, that when I blew my whistle once, the boys were to put the paraffin into the drums stuffed with grass and light them; and when I blew my whistle twice, the cars were to switch on their headlights.

So the aircraft came into the circuit, I heard it, it had its navigation lights on as well; I used my Aldiss lamp as well to indicate I'd got him. I blew my whistle once and the boys dashed around and lit up the drums filled with grass and paraffin, and they were burning nicely so that he could see his nice landing L, and then when he was getting round to his last circuit before the approach, I blew my whistle twice and the cars all switched on their headlights, and lit the area of the landing run. It landed all right, no trouble at all, and everyone was happy.

In fact, it was an RAF aircraft coming down, I don't know how it was that we'd not been notified, but I spoke to the skipper of the aircraft afterwards. He said he'd been told there were no night landing facilities there and to make his own arrangements, but when he made his final approach he said, "the place was lit up, I hadn't seen a place lit up like that since before the war! Certainly not since flying down from England, I've never seen it like that before, even Malta wasn't like that!" You know, so that with the word going round that good old Imperial Airways had done its stuff again, I felt I'd justified my position for the station vis-à-vis the governor and the political party.

We were establishing a very good rapport with the South African Air Force people, not only with the pilots but with the few crews going up and down. This made them happy, because if there was a new bloke, a new pilot on the South African Air Force squadron coming up, he knew he was going to be amongst friends. We used to have quite a lot of fun and real conversation about our problems and their problems and the usual sort of chatter, but it really was a nice arrangement and it became quite a social sort of affair. Obviously not everything was easy, we also had to do a lot of long hours; so many planes arrived in the evening and everything had to get away in the morning, we'd got these passengers always on our hands under conditions which were not ideal. We never had less than eight passengers staying with us, mostly it was considerably more; mostly it was overnight but then we had also the people staying three or four nights, waiting to hear the next communication whether they were going to go north or south or east or west or whichever way they were going. So that we always had passengers on our hands, some disgruntled, some happy.

Mongalla

We also had to check up on the emergency alighting area for the flying boats, that was up at Mongalla. We used to do that trip by road and try to time it so we could come back by river steamer, which made a nice change. There was a track along the east bank of the river, and occasionally in the dry season we did use the track, which was officially a part of the Great North Road which was supposed to be existing between Cape Town and Cairo. It was only a track. And during certain times of the year it was impassable. There was no tarmac or anything it was just soil. Occasionally it used to get so dry we got stuck because of the dusty soil and other times, we had fair rains in and around Juba so it wasn't too bad, normally the surface was all right. But when you got up to Mongalla, you found that the whole of the area was overgrown, and we had to really cut our way through the, almost jungle, to the riverbank in order to be able to check the landing site.

Mongalla had originally been the capital of the Equatoria province, but it had been wiped out; I think it was yellow fever that put paid to that area. They moved the administrative centre down to Juba, and established Juba as the southern port for the steamers. They put the road in down to the Congo and of course the other one they extended down to Nimule to continue what was theoretically the Cape - Cairo road. But we had made this emergency mooring up there, and we occasionally used to go just to check that the emergency mooring buoy was still afloat, because crocodiles seemed to have a habit of trying to sharpen their teeth on the mooring buoys! Or it might of course have caught up a lot of weed going down, and might have taken up with the rubbish which would have built up into sud. So we had to see that clear.

We used to come back overnight on the river steamer if we'd timed it right. We always used to meet the skipper of the river steamer and have a drink with him and a chat about the state of the water and the state of the Nile and matters nautical. One of the army types saw the overgrown state of Mongalla because it was in ruins and rather overgrown and he said: "What happened here, how did it get this way, was it the Italians from Abyssinia?" When I pointed out, no it was yellow fever, he was quite surprised, but he was thinking we'd been raided by air in that area. I think he was feeling quite sorry for us, and he didn't realise of course how dangerous it could be in a yellow fever area.

Church

In spite of the work and the problems there, I found it again a very happy station down in Juba. And although I did my second trip down there I still enjoyed it, I enjoyed the atmosphere and certainly working with the local people and with the native population. There were so few people there it was interesting trying to find out the differences between one tribe and another. I didn't get very successful with that, though, but it was a happy station.

One Saturday the plane came in and there was a woman on it, she was going through to West Africa then going up to join her husband who had been transferred in the Navy, as the Naval Attaché at the embassy in Lisbon, and she was sort of following around to try and catch up with him.

She spoke to me in the Saturday evening. "Do you know if there's a catholic church around?"

"Yes," I said.

"You don't know what time the services are, do you, because I'd like to go?"

"Well, fine, you be on the doorstep at a quarter to seven in the morning and I'll take you."

"Oh, that's very kind of you! All right, thank you."

So in the morning (quarter to seven in those days was not an early hour), quarter to seven I walked across to the part of the hotel she was staying in, met her and then walked round to where the church was. I took her in to the little side entrance which was just that single bench, along the side of the altar, arranged sideways and we attended mass there, seven o'clock.

It was accompanied by singing of course, the local population always sang even at the early morning masses. After mass we walked home.

She said, "you know that didn't do me any good at all."

"What do you mean?"

"Well, just being where we were, we could see all the people in the church, they were all of them black, not another white person there, not another coloured person there, they were all black. And they were all ages, little children running around with nothing on, most of the woman with very little on, the fellows there again, with very little on, and it just seemed odd, that sort of atmosphere, attending mass, the same as I would be attending in an ordinary church where people were sort of restricted in their atmosphere, and they talked, they dressed not only becomingly, they dressed rather smartly because some people thought they should be showing off their best clothes. But to see this almost nude congregation being equally devout, in fact probably far more devout than the congregations in the countries where I normally live, it really was amazing to me, and rather staggering. But then on the other hand it did mean to me that faith and the Catholic church does extend to all nations and all types of people."

I always remember that lass, because you know, I'd never thought of it like that, and she was so happy that there was a church there, and someone to take her, and then to see how the native population behaved and the devotion amongst them. I always remember her name, she was Elizabeth Everitt and her husband was a Lieutenant-Commander who had been posted to the Naval Attaché in Lisbon.

Chapter 18:
Khartoum and Wadi Saidna

At the end of 1941 Geoffrey was posted up to Khartoum. Initially he wasn't very happy, because he would only be Assistant Superintendent rather than the boss, as he had been for some time with his other postings. But there was nothing he could do about it, since he was officially ranked TO2, and there was a TO1 in charge. Khartoum really was a hot place; temperatures there went up to 120 degrees (F) in the shade [about 50°C], and there was no such thing as air conditioning.

I left Juba and moved up to Khartoum, where I found the only accommodation was in the mess. The mess wasn't a Mess, it was the Station Superintendent's house. Because I was sufficiently senior I was in the Station Superintendent's house, and he was in a house that had been taken over under wartime regulations, from an Italian who was being impounded, or detained, because of his nationality. His house then became empty, and Brian Nelson, the Superintendent, who had his wife with him, he'd taken over this glorious house. It was Italian built, and it really was built for the temperatures that Khartoum had, because Khartoum really was a hot place. Brian Nelson was a Welshman, and he had originally been in Burma; he'd been in Airways for about four or five years.

After a very short time working with Brian Nelson at Khartoum station, I got a posting to a new place which was not really on the map, not the Imperial Airways map anyway, a place out in the desert beyond Omdurman, called Wadi Saidna.

This was a new RAF station but it was equally going to be a link station for reinforcement aircraft from West Africa to Sudan, then some up to the Middle East, and others on over Abyssinia to reinforce India, although I didn't know that at the time. I was posted out there to establish communication with the RAF. At the same time the South African Air Force Transport Squadron

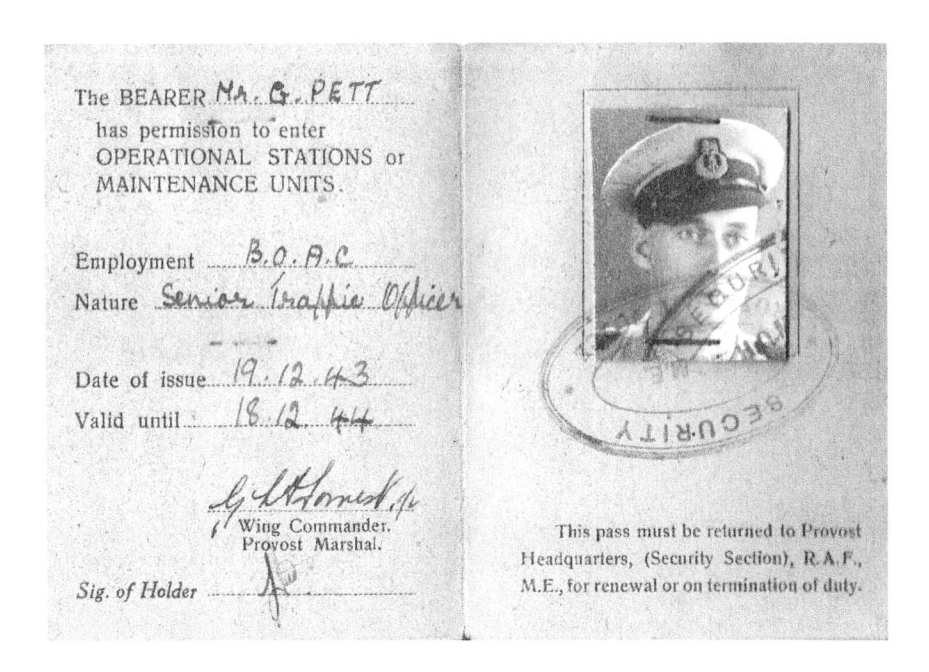

The BEARER M·r· G. PETT
has permission to enter
OPERATIONAL STATIONS or
MAINTENANCE UNITS.

Employment ... B.O.A.C
Nature ... Senior Traffic Officer

Date of issue ... 19.12.43
Valid until ... 18.12.44

Wing Commander,
Provost Marshal.

Sig. of Holder

This pass must be returned to Provost Headquarters, (Security Section), R.A.F., M.E., for renewal or on termination of duty.

decided they would also go to Wadi Saidna and not go into the civil airport at Khartoum, so that when I went out there I had some friends with the SAAF straight away, when they came through. Then I was able to make my contacts and friends within the RAF, who were running the station.

Wadi Saidna had been established earlier; there were many buildings there that were intended as a college for the Sudan government for agricultural training. The RAF had taken over these buildings and scratched the surface of the desert in order to flatten it off, and put a few white stones down there to mark the limits of the cleared area, and there we had a new airport!

I went out to Wadi Saidna having driven across the Nile over to Omdurman and then on a not-marked track to Wadi Saidna. There was only really one lot of marking where the track was and that was two white stones, and I understood before I went out that if you didn't go between the two white stones you were likely to sink in soft sand. That was the only marking of the safe trip out to Wadi Saidna.

For transport, I wanted one of the Ford Land [something], not, as they had in Khartoum, the special so-called tropicalised Wolsey station wagons. I had experience of those when I was working in Khartoum and they were really heavy to drive. Admittedly they had the sand tyres which in those days were a really new thing, but they were so heavy on steering and when you were driving through sand as well it really was murder to try to steer properly. The vehicles had been given over to Imperial Airways for testing by the manufacturers to get reports on how satisfactory they were, as they were trying to open up a market in the tropics for them, but I'm afraid all the comments were that they were completely and totally unsuitable. They used to boil very quickly too, which was another problem where you don't have any water around, it's not as though you could suddenly say 'Oh, top up the radiator', you had to carry water around with you in order to be able to do it. And who wants to pour water in a radiator when you're travelling through arid country and you want water with you to drink.

So instead of having one of those vehicles or the Ford V8 station wagon type which were otherwise available (we had several down in Lindi), the only thing I could get was the 19 horsepower four cylinder Ford. I think it was a 1929 model, it was really as sort of 'sit up and beg' type of car, in fact it was exactly the same as my Miranda that I had had on holiday when I went home in 1939. So I was very familiar with it, but how it would work in the desert conditions I had no idea. That was the only vehicle I could acquire so I took that and it was most satisfactory as a vehicle. I never really had any trouble; there was only once or twice that I ever got into trouble and that was a blocked petrol feed. But then it was a gravity tank and the fluid just went down the tube into the base of the tank into the carburettor, so it was a very simple thing to turn off the petrol in the gravity tank, and then detach the tube, blow through the tube, and then re-attach the tubes, turn the taps on the gravity tank and try your luck. And sure enough it worked! That was the only trouble I had with that vehicle even though I went frequently across the desert from and to Wadi Saidna - six miles across desert all the way. I was so glad that I'd originally had Miranda and knew how to handle it, and this one was just as good as Miranda had been.

Having met the Wing Commander in charge of Wadi Saidna station I was allocated a bungalow for myself right on the edge of the camp, which to me was very useful. It meant that I was living on my own a bit, but I was able to eat in the officer's mess. I had my own quarters and I had my servant looking after the place, cleaning etc. and of course doing my dhobi. So that life was reasonably pleasant - except for the heat.

When I got out there, there were no Imperial Airways operations and the only plane operating was when SAAF Transport Squadron transferred from Khartoum to the RAF station and that came up from Juba through Malakal to Wadi Saidna. So I then had pilots and crew that I knew coming through from South Africa, whom I had known when I was down in Juba, so that was a pleasant contact with old friends.

Pan-American

The Pan-American airline had formed themselves a new company called Pan-America Africa Ltd and they had been awarded the contract by the American government to arrange the delivery of aircraft from the States out to the Far East. After a few months I found the RAF had allocated a couple of blocks to Pan-American Ltd and also a couple of office blocks, and we were waiting for when Pan-America Africa Ltd would be starting its job.

I heard, through RAF communications, that two Dakotas were coming over from West Africa with the initial personnel for Pan-American. That plane landed and what do we find? We find half a dozen fellows on one aeroplane and on the next aeroplane absolutely everything in the way of air-conditioning and cooking and feeding. Air-conditioning was the first thing – they wouldn't move any other staff except these initial six people into the area until they'd got air-conditioning in both residential blocks and the offices. This really was a shattering thing because living out there, to us, we really didn't know about air-conditioning. It really caused a laugh because we were all used to adapting to the heat and we realised that if they were going to get themselves mollycoddled in these air-conditioned blocks, when they had to go out into the "fresh" air, they would be really suffering. They would probably find it incapacitated them so much that they'd either decide they had to give up the air-conditioning or they'd be shipped back home after short periods. I subsequently discovered that the staff were only posted out to Wadi Saidna for a three-month tour and then they went back home again.

The mail

In the meantime, of course, I had settled down in a routine way of living out there in the desert. The SAAF squad coming through meant that I had at least something of my own responsibility because they always carried mail.

The mail they brought up had to go through to Khartoum and this meant I had to arrange some sort of transport. I was able to sort out not only an ex-army three ton truck but also a couple of guys on the staff of Imperial Airways Khartoum as drivers.

We used to have one driver based at Wadi Saidna the whole time, and they alternated. Rather than stay right in camp, he was accommodated in a native quarter alongside the river which was the original planned accommodation for the native staff under the Sudan Government original plan. I had to send this man into Khartoum in the afternoon after the arrival of the South African aircraft with its mail, and I found that there were a number of the RAF lads that had passes, who would be very keen to go into Khartoum but they had no transport. So I arranged with the Wing Commander in charge that if any of the fellows had out-of-camp passes they would be allowed on my truck; it would pick them up at the guard post on the outside of the camp and, providing they were approved by the governor of the guard, they would be allowed on my truck to Khartoum. But I set it up so that the truck would leave at half past eleven at night, after the cinema and most of the clubs had closed, so that at least the lads could have an evening in town, and my driver could have at least some time with his family in Khartoum and then come back that night. I had this rule published through the camp: first, only those that had passes could be picked up at the camp gate (having been approved by the officer in charge of the guard) and second, that they would have to be at the terminal for the truck coming back at 11.30; they would be left behind if they weren't there on time. My driver had strict orders that he must leave on time and he was to ignore any calls to pick up pals etc. Actually this went off very well, and over the few weeks or so everybody was very happy. In fact it did me a lot of good, as this was really the only way that any of the lads could get into Khartoum. It gave them the opportunity to go to a show or a NAAFI thing or visit one of the nightclubs or go to a bar or whatever they wanted to do in the evening. Being able to avail themselves of my van gave me a great amount of kudos.

It was particularly reflected on one particular day just before the SAAF plane was due in; there was a flight of aircraft come into Wadi Saidna in transit up to the Western Desert as reinforcement aircraft. Naturally, the reinforcement aircraft had priority over all the other operations, and it meant all the refuelling gangs were fully tied up until the aircraft of the reinforcement flight were off again, or at least completely refuelled. There were no available gangs to refuel the SAAF plane.

So when the South Africans got in and saw what was ahead

of them, and I explained the position to the skipper, he said, "well, is there anything you can do?" and I said "I don't know; I think there might be."

I went and had a word with the flight sergeant and said, "you realise I want to get this plane away as well, but I know you've got priority on the reinforcement flights, but if you could let me have the petrol somehow I'll get the people on the South African plane to refuel themselves."

He replied, "well, I've got a bowser available, so if you can get them to refuel themselves that'll be fine, they can get on with it."

So I said "Right!" and I went and talked to the skipper, who said "Yay, that's all right we can do that."

All his passengers were South African army or air-force personnel, so the skipper detailed some of the passengers and his crew to get the bowser, connect it up and start pumping in. The pumping in was done by the old-fashioned hand wobble pump, so it was quite a job for people that weren't used to it. Nevertheless, the skipper was able to sign for the fuel, the bowser was safely taken away from the aircraft, and he got away without having to be delayed to the end of the reinforcement flight.

Now if it hadn't have been for my having the availability for the transport for the lads into Khartoum, the goodwill wouldn't have been there, and I wouldn't have the opportunity of being able to get the South African Air Force planes away.

Meeting these planes was quite amusing at times because the plane would come down and, having flown at around 5-6,000 feet, the cabin was nice and cool! Well, this was the funny thing about it, the aircraft would land, the door would open, with myself going towards the door I sort of felt an icy blast come out, whereas the people trying to get out just walked into a wall of heat! This was quite well experienced from my point of view, which was why I wouldn't go into the cabin and get frozen for a few minutes and then come out again into the heat. So, in work with the SAAF I always stayed outside the aircraft, I never went inside. But I remember one time the passenger coming out made a comment

saying something like:
"How can you cope with this sort of thing, this heat?"
And I said, "well, you know, it's not very hot."
He said: "way! what do you mean, it's not very hot?"
"Well, the temperature's only about 110 [42C] at the moment."
"How do you cope with that, what does it go up to?"
"Well, I do have to do weather reports and the highest so far that I've had to report was 128 in the shade." [55C]
I won't tell you what he said!

Desert, sea and air manoeuvres

There was of course the other side of it. While we were there, we had a number of companies of troops for desert training or *tropicalisation* or whatever term they used. They were sent out to Wadi Saidna for training on desert tactics and the like.

They lived under canvas, so to start with that was a pretty warm job. These lads were out, rushing around, fighting, doing manoeuvres, at between 10 and 12 in daylight with full kit; this to me was absolute murder! How they coped I do not know. I was *conditioned* to at least be able to walk around, but there were these lads having just straight come out from UK, having been shipped out to West Africa and then flown across from West Africa to Khartoum, posted out to Wadi Saidna for desert training. I don't know, I sort of sympathised with them. Some of the training officers used to go frequently into Khartoum, and I said I felt sorry for these lads having to do this sort of thing under those conditions. But as the officers said, it's all part of the training and they have to go up and fight in these sort of conditions in the Western Desert so if we can get them trained for these conditions they'll be so much more proficient as soldiers. And I suppose that's right, but just to hear and see them thrashing about in those hours in the morning, it made me thank God I was a civilian.

Subsequently, I happened to meet some of the fellows who had been through Wadi Saidna in battle training and desert training. Talking to them, they all of them said, although they cursed the training they had to undergo when they were out at Wadi Saidna, when they were up in the Western Desert to them it was comparatively a piece of cake. They were able to cope with the conditions up in the Western Desert and the fighting conditions so much easier because they had experienced the conditions down in Khartoum. They were much better off than the other lads that didn't get that training and had been put up in the conditions in the Western Desert without any 'desertisation' to start with.

Progress on my personal life

It seems a long time ago that I mentioned my fiancée and the hiatus of the Italians coming into the war in June 1940 which not only stopped us being able to get together out in Alexandria but cut us off except for the routine mail we were able to exchange. During our correspondence, we realised that it was going to be a long time before I was likely to get back to England enabling us to get married, so Frances was examining the possibilities of being posted to Africa and us getting together. She worked very well as a nurse and was also a qualified midwife. She found that if she joined the Overseas Nursing Service, she would be allowed out of the country, whereas if she stayed as a civilian nurse she would never be able to get out. The other way would be to join one of the forces' nursing branches, but she would be drafted and she would never know where she would be posted. So she decided to apply for the Overseas Nursing Service and then take any offer that seemed likely to lead to a posting where we might be able to get married.

The Overseas Nursing Service accepted her and the first posting she was offered was to the Bahamas or something like that. And of course all her friends said, lovely, terrific posting, you must take that! But of course if she'd taken that it wouldn't get her anywhere near me, and we'd be further away than ever before. She turned that one down and the next one she was offered was Singapore, and thank God she didn't take that, otherwise she'd have gone out there and gone pretty much straight into the prison camps. Anyway, she didn't take that and I think she was offered another which was miles away, and she was warned that if she didn't take the next one then she'd be taken off the Overseas Nursing List and revert to being a civilian nurse. So she had her fingers crossed, but the one she was offered was for Uganda. All her friends thought, terrible place to go, you can't go there, but she shrugged her shoulders, and hid her smiles, and said, oh well, I'll have to take it. She was very pleased to be able to take Uganda, although exactly where Uganda was relative to me was a bit vague: she knew it was in Africa, but that was about the lot.

When I heard she was coming out to Uganda I was able to indicate to her that it was reasonably proximate and that was a good thing to have done! Then I had a scare when Maxwell [Director, Cairo] started talking about posting me back to the UK. I sent a signal to Frances saying, hold it, don't come out because I might be coming home! By that time, it was far too late for her to make any cancellation; she had to come out anyway. Fortunately, Maxwell's plan transferring me to the UK – I don't know why he wanted to transfer me, and I don't know what happened to stop me being transferred - it all fell through. Frances hadn't done anything about stopping her posting out to Uganda, and during the early part of '42 she left the UK.

She was coming out by boat convoy, so nobody knew when she would leave or what route she would take, and how she would get anywhere. All I could do to help in case she got into difficulty or wanted some help was to write to all the Station Superintendents at the various stations around the African coast that she might have to call into. I told them if Frances (Mollie) Hutchinson called in there, she was a nurse coming round to East Africa, and if she called in to them and asked for help, would they please give her any help that was necessary and then refer any expense for it back to me. This was quite a normal thing we used to do in peace time; quite often you would get a piece of paper saying 'my aunt - or my sister or my brother-in-law - was travelling over on such and such a flight and if would you give her a hand we'd be grateful'; it was done within the family of Imperial Airways. So when I did it I didn't see anything different, it was a normal thing for it to happen. I didn't know where the boats went, so I sent these messages out to all the stations around the west coast of Africa, starting with, I think it was Kakarati, then all stations south to Cape Town, then all stations north to Mombasa, Nairobi and Kampala. So if she wanted any help she could have got in touch with any of the station superintendents of those places. I don't think she got in touch with any of them, thank God, because that meant everything was safely under control. Subsequently I found that she had a pleasant trip out, but there was the possibility that something might go wrong and at least I'd laid the carpet out so that she could bounce on it instead of getting hurt.

There was in fact a very real possibility of something going wrong. When I was at Wadi Saidna the SAAF boys did a couple of trips up on the Transport Squadron then went back to their usual routine, which at the time was light bombers or either Blenheims or Lockheeds doing maritime patrol. They knew there were three, positively two but possibly three Japanese submarines wandering around the Madagascar coast, or between South Africa, Mozambique and Madagascar, around the Madagascar Channel. As the Madagascar Channel was the way the boat would be coming up from South Africa to East Africa I was very interested!

They knew of my interest, and one of the times the skipper came up he said: "Oh I've got a message for you."

"Oh really?"

"Yes, apparently a lass called in, in Durban, and it got through to us. She's coming up to Uganda and they mentioned your name as well, so we thought we'd better pass it on to you that she has got to Durban. She'll be leaving Durban and coming up to Mombasa by the East Coast boat service."

That was the first time I'd got any information, and knowing that, and knowing what they were doing about looking for the Japanese subs in the Madagascar Channel, I had a little time holding my breath.

By the time Frances got through to Uganda, I'd been transferred from Wadi Saidna up to Cairo. It seemed that whenever we tried to get together, something went wrong, not only did Italy come into the war in '40, but Maxwell sent me out of the Sudan up to Egypt, further away from her, as soon as she arrived in Uganda.

The boat she was on was reportedly in the last convoy to get through. Frances heard while she was nursing in Kampala that a sub had sunk it in the Indian Ocean. Her sad comment when she told the story to her family years later was "all those boys..."

Chapter 19:
Cairo and Kampala

In Cairo, I took over as Senior Traffic Operator at Cairo Station. That meant I was responsible for all the traffic handling and organisation for the station which covered of course not only Rod El Farag the flying boat station, but the land plane base at Heliopolis and the new station we'd opened up at Cairo West, which was out beyond the Pyramids and was the station for serving the Western Desert.

Throughout that year, I corresponded with Frances who was settling herself down in the nursing organisation in Kampala. I was trying to settle myself down in Cairo, because if I wanted to get married and bring her up to Cairo (or bring her up to Cairo and get married) I *had* to have accommodation. This was one of the immigration rules, that any women coming in had to have accommodation and any wives joining husbands, the husbands had to have suitable accommodation for their wives to join them. I took over a flat in Gezira for the other lads that were working out there, so instead of having to maintain the mess, which was originally on the *west* side of the island, so therefore inundated by the noise from the nightclubs on the river bank, this flat that I rented was on the other bank. It was much more accessible into Cairo Office but it also gave us better access to the Gezira Club which was where all of us used to spend most of our off-duty time. There was me, Alistair Thomson, Oliver Hove, Keith Cockerell, just the four of us, and it was a four bedroom flat which was very useful, quite apart from the dining room and bathroom.

We spent whatever spare time we had at the Gezira Club doing either squash or tennis or swimming; swimming of course very frequently, or just sitting under the shade of the trees and having tea or a cold drink! We used to meet a lot of fellows and of course a lot of girls! Most of the girls were daughters of the

Government officials who lived and were brought up in Cairo because their fathers were Egyptian Government officials although they were English fellows. These lasses used to talk to us occasionally, and we'd take them to the dance at Gezira Club. We socialised generally, which made the lads very happy of course. But on one occasion we found that the lasses weren't government girls or Cairo girls, they were in fact Wrens (WRNS). One of them was saying that they weren't quite certain whether they were going to stay the night because they had three or four days leave from Alexandria down in Cairo, but they hadn't been able to get into any of the Wrens' accommodation.

"Well," we said, "we've got one spare room, and if you don't mind sharing the accommodation you can move in there."

"No, you can't do that sort of thing!" they said.

"Well, it's all right. We're used to having our own staff move in and move out, so it's just the same."

"Could you really?"

I think one of the lads was away, so that we had the spare room. So, we took them up to our mess and they just used that room, had breakfast with us the next morning, and then they spent their day doing what they wanted to do.

When they were leaving, they asked, "how much do we owe you for messing?"

"That's all right, we enjoyed your company; but you could bring us some cigarettes or some tobacco when you next come." And they said they'd do that.

The next thing that happened was a phone call from some Wren who was coming to Cairo and asked if she could use our accommodation and she would bring a tin of tobacco. There were two of us, Oliver and myself who smoked pipes, the rest smoked cigarettes, so Oliver and I got tins of navy pipe tobacco and it was good stuff! The best smokes we had for years during the war! Several Wrens, in pairs, came and stayed in one of the rooms in our mess when one of the fellows was away, and it really was a change and it was amusing, and it was lovely having that tobacco!

Throughout this period, I was trying to organise a trip for myself down to Kampala to get married. Maxwell seemed to frustrate every effort that I made. He set up a rule about 'not being able to take leave in other than a 'house resort' or 'health station' he called it. 'Health station' was something that Maxwell defined himself, and he only referred to Teheran as being a health station and never considered anything else, ruling out any possibility of me being able to go down to Uganda. Then we had the reinforcement of the Western Desert and the Middle East generally, plus the armed forces feeding through Cairo to the Far East for the Burmese campaign using our Horseshoe Route, which of course meant that all channels of transportation were completely priority booked. Maxwell used that to indicate that we couldn't have civilians coming out and saying they had priority. So, I had to settle down as best I could to getting on working and doing the best job - in the job - and trying to forget about the fact that I had problems on the personal side. In fact, we were working very hard, and with the possibility of Rommel breaking through on the Libyan borders into Egypt we were also having to consider the possibility of having to evacuate Cairo.

Cairo evacuation plans

One of my jobs during that period was to assess the options for evacuating the air operations from Cairo. The basis we were working on was a report by Douglas Grey who did a car trip from Cairo through to Aqaba in the Arabian Gulf to plan the possible evacuation of Cairo, using Aqaba as the turning point on our Horseshoe Route between South Africa and Australia, West Africa and Australia, and West Africa and South Africa. That would make Aqaba a real junction point for the airlines. If we had to get out of Cairo, it was felt Aqaba was probably the most suitable place, but of course Aqaba was completely desert.

As required, I drew up plans for the evacuation of Cairo, which included transport of vital things straight away in order to establish a base for the 'boats to fly across and build up the movement of the boats there. We had to put a primary station down first, which was similar to what I had to do when I moved from Butiaba up to Juba. The transport problem was an absolute shocker; some of the photographs that Douglas Grey had incorporated in his report of the trip really made one's hair stand on end.

I did a lot of work in preparing for the evacuation of Cairo. We placed the equipment that we would take with us in strategic places so that, if it happened, vehicles would be available, and this stuff we were taking with us would also be available, and we would waste no time dashing around trying to collect bits and pieces. We then settled down to wait and see what happened, carrying on our normal working.

Of course, after the Battle of El Alamein, the idea of the evacuation of Cairo was dropped and we got back to normal working. Except, with the success in the Western Desert, we increased our civilian flights from the airport out of Cairo West with Lockheeds out to the Western Desert, moving up just behind the front line as it captured more territory. Of course, we carried on our normal operation of the Horseshoe Route and we were also operating an ordinary air service with Lockheeds up to Teheran from Cairo.

A little side trip

I was still looking around for suitable accommodation so I could think of getting married. Frances was still down in Kampala carrying on her work. I don't know whether she was thinking of coming up or whether she was just enjoying herself down in Kampala! In the middle of March 1943, I was granted three weeks local leave as a result of the time that I'd spent without any leave at all. This was obviously the time to get myself down to Kampala and organise things down there. By that time, fortunately, I had been able to rent a flat in Gezira that I hoped would be suitable for a married couple, so I did my planning to try to get down and get married.

There was quite a lot of amusement about this, because the staff around knew jolly well that Maxwell had been objecting to my getting married and objecting to me going down to Kampala, which of course was outside his area of control, and wasn't what he called a health station. Then he put a ban on me using our own flights as well, so people thought I really was in trouble! But my usual friends, the South African Air Force chaps, they rallied round and I was offered a place down south from Cairo. With just a local leave [permit] I started off by being taken by the South African Air Force Transport Squadron southbound as far as they could take me. Actually, they took me all the way and I arrived in Kampala about midday on the 22nd March. I checked in at the Imperial Hotel saying I'd be there just a few days, then I went down to the hospital to find Frances, who was still known as Mollie then, went down to check up and find out if she was still willing to say 'yes'.

At the hospital I was told she was on night duty; she was over at the nurses' home sleeping, as she'd come off duty earlier on that day. But as it was early afternoon by that time, I went down to the nurses' home and explained to the receptionist there that I wanted to see her. Apparently, she told Frances that there was a 'gentleman in uniform asking for her at the entrance'. Frances was reported to have said, "he'll have to wait, I'm sleeping," but was persuaded to come along. Of course when she saw me, not knowing that I was going to be there, it was a huge shock!

We then discussed the possibility of carrying on to get married but she was going on duty in a short time so we arranged that I would meet her the following morning when she came off duty, before she went and had her sleep, to try to work out the details of how we would get ourselves fixed up.

The next day I went down to the Celtic church to see the local priest, who I found was a White Father [a Catholic missionary order] named Father Hughes. We had a chat and he asked when I wanted to get married, and I said "by the end of the week!"

And he sort of giggled and said, "you don't really mean that."

And I said "Yes I do, I've only got a fourteen day leave and I want to get married and go off on our honeymoon and then I have to get back up to Cairo."

So he appreciated that but said: "you'll of course need a special licence."

I could see there were many obstacles still, but asked, "well where do I get that from?"

"You'll have to apply through the local district office to get the Governor to sign it, and if you want a nuptial mass, I'll have to get permission from the Archbishop in Nairobi, because of course this is during Lent."

So that really started a bit of panic, but we hoped everything would work out. I was able to tell Frances that things were working, but I couldn't indicate what day we'd be likely to get married. I was hoping that as things were starting to work out, it would probably be at least a week before we got the permissions through and could arrange the ceremony.

We did eventually get the licences. For the special licence, I went along to the district officer who took my details down and checked my passport. He knew Frances as she was a nursing sister in the hospital and he accepted our planning, but the Governor, who had to sign the special licence, was on safari doing a tour! I'd have to hire a runner to be able to take the licence out to him, catch up with him, get him to sign it and the runner bring the licence back again! So there was at least two days lost in the runner going out and coming back.

Hiring a runner was quite a known thing about that period of the administration. You'd get this runner, he'd go to deliver his message but he always carries a stick which is a split in the end, and the message or envelope or whatever it was would be slid in this split cane. When he was running along (or walking, or trotting, going along however he'd go) he would be given priority under all circumstances because he was a runner on official business.

I remember earlier on, when I was down in Mbeya, that at one time I was out in the car and I saw a lad running along with his cleft stick with his message at the end of it. I stopped and asked him where he was going and he told me, so I said "Well, ok, I'm going there" so I picked him up and drove him along and I dropped him where he wanted to go. And when he got off he said "Thank you very much" and was very grateful, but would I give him back the rest of his day? Now this fluffed me, I didn't know what he really meant. Subsequently I found that his view was that he normally would have arrived at that destination in the late afternoon of the day, whereas I was dropping him there at midday. So therefore I had stolen the time from midday to the evening, which he would normally be travelling, I'd stolen that time from him because I'd delivered him early.

Anyway, things were working; Father Hughes had sent off his request for permission for the nuptial mass and the runner had gone off with the licence, so things were working out, and it was rather a question of fixing the day for the wedding. The special licence for which I paid £5, number 206, was signed by the Governor dated the 27th March 1943, and it accepted that I could get married under that licence within seven days of the date of the licence. I had to plan as much as possible on knowing that I had to get back to Cairo so that I could report back at the end of my leave on the 11th April, which was the first day I had to be back working, in other words my leave terminated on 10th April. And I really did have to worry about getting back to Cairo, as everything northbound was priority traffic. I had previously made an arrangement with a flying boat pilot, that he would come and pick me up at Laropi, so I had to see the emigration and health people to get permission to be picked up there because Laropi was in a prohibited health area and it wasn't an official port! This was fine and I'd anticipated that would happened somewhere around the 6th, 7th or 8th of the month. I remember that the passport I was using at the time had that special endorsement in it by the health people and also the emigration people saying 'permitted to be uplifted up from Laropi in Uganda'.

I'd been busy with the plans that I'd made with the government official and the church, but Frances was busy with her stuff of course! She wanted to get a dress for the occasion, she wanted to make sure the hospital staff weren't too inconvenienced by her wanting to take some time off for the wedding and of course for a few days honeymoon! So she was very busy because she was doing her normal nursing duty and making plans. When she came off-duty and before she went to sleep we used to have a chat and get ourselves up to date. We were talking about a honeymoon, and the problems with that were the trains through Kampala, which only operated eastbound on the Friday and westbound on a Saturday. It was the same train actually, it went eastbound as far as Rwenzori and terminated there and came back through Kampala the next day. As a result, I made up my mind that if we got married on the Friday we'd get the train and go up to the Mountains of the Moon, which I thought sounded romantic, and so I suggested to Frances that we got married on the 1st April. This I thought was a convenient date, I'd always remember the date I was married! But she said, oh she couldn't do that, not that she was worried about the date of the 1st April, but because she would not be able to do all the work of the reorganisation of the nursing schedule and so on in time. But she could do it for Saturday 2nd, so that really fixed that we would have the wedding on the 2nd providing we got all the permissions. Father Hughes was happy about that as if we didn't get the permissions through, he could still marry us, it just wouldn't be a nuptial mass.

David Paton, the station superintendent of Imperial Airways down in Kampala, was the only person I knew down there, so I left socialising side to Frances. But her knowledge of people there was restricted to the nursing fraternity. We were not having anything elaborate in the way of our wedding, just the nuptial mass - we weren't going to have a major reception afterwards as we hadn't got the number of people there anyway to do it with. But for any wedding mass at all, we would of course fast before communion, so after the wedding ceremony what we really wanted was some breakfast, it was the first time we'd have something to eat! So I arranged with the hotel that we would have a wedding breakfast, which would be just an ordinary breakfast from the menu of the hotel. Some people thought it was rather extraordinary. I remember David Paton making some comment subsequently, that we didn't even have any champagne! Whoever had champagne with breakfast anyway? The mass was going to be at 8 o'clock, we didn't want it later on when the heat was really stoking up, we had it in the morning at a reasonable time.

On the morning of the wedding I walked down from the hotel to the Church of Christ the King which was the Catholic church in Kampala. I found a flight lieutenant in uniform who asked, "Are you Geoffrey Pett" so I said yes, and he said "I'm Morris Walter, I'm your best man." That was the first time I met him! I don't know who organised him but apparently he was the Met Officer at the RAF station there and it didn't worry me at all, if he was to be the official witness that was grand! Frances of course had a Lady in Waiting, it was one of the wives there, Mrs McHugh. I don't know what her first name was. So we had two official witnesses, Flight Lt. Walter and Mrs McHugh. Quite honestly, I don't remember if there was anybody other than David Paton and the two official witnesses there. I'm sure there must have been one or two other people there but I can't remember who they were.

Because we were getting married on the Saturday, we couldn't go to the Mountains of the Moon; we'd have to go in the other direction, because we didn't want to stay in Kampala. The nearest place that I thought might be suitable was in Jinja. I didn't know what it was like; we had to take everything as we found it. I rang the hotel in Jinja and booked a room, and then after the ceremony we packed ourselves up, and got onto the train and went down to Jinja. It was a lovely little hotel.

It was on the road along the waterways where the water tumbles out of Lake Victoria at Owen Stanley Falls, which run up to Lake Kirga, which then carries on westbound and goes into the Murchison Falls and tumbles down into the Albert Nile. That earlier part of it is called Victoria Nile.

One or two things I remember about being in that hotel is firstly the sound of the natives walking past. When there were several of them going about their business they used to chant; you had this wonderful African chant, it really was most impressive. The other thing that Frances noticed most particularly was the hippos. There were quite a lot of hippos in the waterways around there and they used to snort during the night and used to wake her up with this snorting! They used to wander close up to the hotel and almost walk in through the windows, and snorting just outside the hotel! And the other thing that I remember too was the table at breakfast time, on the table was a vase of white gardenias, which I thought was very nice of the hotel people to have done that for us!

Actually the gardenias were growing around in the garden of the hotel so it was only a case of picking them, but you know, to particularly pick the white gardenias and make a little spray of them on our breakfast table I thought was very kind.

Return to Cairo

After our five days honeymooning we had to get back, well I had to get back because I'd only allowed myself three days to get from Kampala back up to Cairo otherwise I'd be overstaying my leave. We went back to Kampala and it was then that I got a real blow. I got a message through from Lagos via David Paton, the station superintendent at Kampala, saying the skipper who had kindly said he would make an experimental landing at Laropi in order to "check the facilities" said he wouldn't be on the service, so it wouldn't be happening. That rather stymied my plans. I had to scratch my head to work out how to get back up to Cairo now that my original plan had failed. It was impossible to stay in Kampala because I knew there was a shortage of frequency and there were already passengers for Imperial Airways queuing, priority ones that had been offloaded were sitting in Kampala waiting to get up, and one of the people who was waiting to carry on going northbound was Maxwell's wife! I met her before I got married when I was in the Imperial Hotel; she had been there a couple of days when I arrived southbound. She was still waiting when I got back after the honeymoon. As she still hadn't got away, my chances would be nil out of Kampala.

I decided that the best thing was to get up to Juba where I knew there were far more aircraft around and moving through, so a much better chance of being able to do something. Was there a taxi that could take me up to Juba? Now the air distance from Kampala to Juba is around 300 miles, but the road journey on the tracks one had to use would be, I don't know, more like 450 miles, so trying to get a taxi to do the journey was a little bit difficult. Eventually I did get a taxi fellow who was willing to take me through, and we knew it would take us two days to make the journey, so I then had to pack up and kiss my wife goodbye after having been married for five or six days, not knowing when I would see her again.

We shared the driving, the taxi man and myself on this journey; you couldn't expect one man to drive all by himself. It was very difficult driving. It was a beaten track, an earth road, it wasn't even gravel, but it was earth solidly packed down by the heavy lorries that the Uganda Railways Transport used. But there were also ferries that you had to cross, and these ferries were just a barge with ropes attached so that you pulled yourself across. If it was over the other side when you got there you had to pull it back to your side, drive onto the ferry and then with the pulley ropes you had to pull yourself across and then drive away. This happened four or five times before we got to a night stop. There were no hotels on the road, there were no towns on the journey at all, but there was this Government resthouse like the one described on the journey from Butiaba to Juba, when we moved the station. We stayed in this Government resthouse for the night, and the next day we drove on, each taking turns to drive, until we eventually arrived in Juba.

When I came to pay the taxi driver the money that he'd told me it would cost, I said "You'll take a cheque will you?" and he said "Oh no, no, no."

No, he wouldn't take a cheque, he was going into Juba and he knew I was going from Juba up to Cairo as quick as I could get away and the idea of taking a cheque from somebody not only that he didn't know but was dashing out of civilisation almost, was unacceptable. So I said all right, drive me down to the Indian dooka (he wasn't an Indian dooka he was Greek actually), so he drove me down to the shop. It was about the only reasonable shop there was in Juba. I went in there with the driver, and the boss there, Crassus, Panioti Crassus his name was, said "oh, Mr Pett, fancy seeing you, where have you been?" and went on for a while. I told him I'd just come up from Kampala by taxi and I'd got to pay the taxi but I hadn't got any cash and I wondered if he'd cash a cheque for me. And he said "Oh yes!"

It was quite a large sum, and I wrote out the cheque and gave it to him, and he counted out the money and gave it to me, and I handed it over to the English driver who wouldn't trust another English man because I was leaving the country! Panioti Crassus, he trusted me all right, no trouble at all, but the driver that I'd been with a couple of days, he wouldn't trust me at all.

I don't remember who was in charge of Juba at the time, it was either Alan Watts or Oliver Hove, one or the other, but in any case, they made no bones about the fact it was going to be 'a bit difficult to get me away'. The next day a Sabena flight came in. I knew the Sabena pilot, of course, and he was terminating at Khartoum and he took me as supernumerary crew up to Khartoum. But having arrived at Khartoum, my friend George Boughton was in charge there, and when I told him about getting back, I found he knew; everybody knew about me and Maxwell and trying to get married!

I told him, "I've got two days to get back to Cairo or I'll have overstayed my leave."

"You haven't got a hope in hell, we've got a whole list of priority people waiting here for transport to Cairo, by the train too." There was a train service up to Cairo, by train and boat, up through the river north of Sudan and into Egypt. "The train service also has got a week's backlog of traffic, you haven't got a hope."

So I thought, oh well, but said, "I'll tell you what, will you get one of the lads to run me out to Wadi Saidna, I'll see what I can do out there."

"Well, you'll have the same trouble out there," he said. "Why not stay here comfortably?"

But I said I'd try Wadi Saidna, so he let me have one of his vans and a driver, and he drove me out to Wadi Saidna, where I saw their local air transport officer, and told him my problem. He said he'd got three fellows that wanted to get up, and he'd see what he could do for me, but he didn't see much hope. If I'd take short notice then that would be fine. And I said provided I could get away then I'd go. But he was a fellow that remembered me from when I was working at Wadi Saidna, so I got a bed in one of the messes and tucked myself down to go to sleep. I was roughly awakened at three o'clock in the morning by one of the airman, saying "Can you come now, because the duty officer says we can get you away if you can come in the next half hour."

So I said "Right!" and I was up and dressed and out.

The duty officer said, "It's the only thing we can do, it's in a Boston, a flight of Bostons going through, delivering up to the Western Desert, we've got one seat that's available in the Boston."

"I don't mind, thank you very much!"

It was a flight of three, and I was allowed on one of them, which happened fortunately to be the flight leader's aircraft. I had to go on as crew, of course, because there were no passenger seats in the Boston bomber, but the position I had to take was the bomb aimer's! I slid into the belly of this aircraft lying on my tummy all the way up to Cairo! This was rather fun because although there was no oxygen and no heating, there was an intercom point so at least I was able to put on the headphones and listen to what was going on. But I didn't realise, of course, and I only had my tropical uniform and flying up at about 10,000 feet, we didn't go higher than that thank goodness, but going along at 10,000 feet it was very very cold indeed!

But I was safely going ahead.

Then I heard that one of the aircraft was in trouble and he was going to have to land at the next emergency landing place. The three of us circled round, and the one in trouble landed down at this emergency landing base. The skipper, Myercroft who was the leader, radioed off indicating to the control centre that this fellow had landed safely, and his position. Then we went off again; we landed at Luxor and refuelled, and then took off again. Well, we started circling again and I listened on the intercom and heard the second aircraft was in trouble and going to land at an emergency place; so we circled round while he landed and he landed safely, and I thought oh, no, no *please*! Because this was the last day you see, I had to get up to Cairo so that I could report tomorrow! And fortunately we did get through. We landed at Heliopolis and I was able to hitch a lift with Imperial Airways transport into Cairo.

Much to the amazement of the people there on the following morning, I turned up ready for duty as the Assistant Traffic Superintendent, Near East Region. The first thing I did was to go up to Maxwell's office and see his secretary, who said "Oh I heard you were back!"

"How did you hear I was back?"

"Oh (so-and-so) told me they saw you."

So I said, "well, is he in?" meaning Maxwell, and she said, "no he's not in yet."

This was about nine o'clock so I waited for him and he came in about half past nine, and his secretary said there's someone to see you. And I went in.

Poor old Maxwell, he was absolutely shattered that I was there reporting on time, but I made it even worse by saying, "Oh by the way, your wife asked me to give you her best wishes and to say she's still on her way."

"Where did you see her then?"

"Well, she was down in Kampala when I was down there."

"But that was three days ago!"

I said, "Yes, she's been down there for weeks but she hasn't been able to get away."

"But you got away?"

"Yes. I told you a long time ago, if I couldn't get up and down Africa where I've travelled before, why did you employ me as a man in the airlines? So, no, she couldn't make it, but I made it all right."

There was quite a bit of amusement among the staff that I'd got down to Kampala and I'd got myself married but most importantly that I'd got back on time to report to Maxwell right on the dot. Most people didn't think I'd make it and Maxwell didn't think I'd possibly make it, particularly when he found how his wife got stuck anyway. All right, I stuck my neck out saying I'd had the experience up and down the routes and if I couldn't make it nobody could, but fortunately I proved myself right. Mind you, I only made it by buying the taxi ride from Kampala up to Juba. If I hadn't been able to get that taxi ride, I don't know how I'd have made it, but still! I made it, and that's the end of it.

Chapter 20:
The end of the story

So I got back up to Cairo and then had to start thinking about my work. I was then Assistant Traffic Superintendent, Near East Region and had the responsibilities to the Traffic Superintendent for all sorts of things for the area up from the Western Desert out to Teheran and from Alexandria down to Juba and all stations on that section. It was all part of the routine, to me it was routine anyway, we worked hard, we had to do time at nighttime as duty officers, for emergency stuff that might happen during the night, but that was the life. At the same time I was wondering how I could get Frances up to Cairo to join me. Although she was now a wife, a wife travelling would have very low priority on the priorities board, where military requirements meant that priorities became the first requirement. But I just had to try and hope for the best amongst my friends in airways.

In correspondence with Frances I found that she would have to give notice to the Uganda Government to terminate her service in the Nursing Service because she was on a three-year contract. I hadn't anticipated that! So she wouldn't be able to leave at a moment's notice if I got the priority or got some sort of wangle fixed. She would have to give notice and if I hadn't got it sorted by that time, she would just have to sit around waiting till I got one. I don't quite know how I fixed it but she eventually got away. I had a payment to make to the Uganda Government to buy her out of her contract: I always remember that because it was the equivalent of eight cows! Later if we were talking to anybody socially, when the opportunity arose I used to say "yes, well, she cost me eight cows," and it always went down with a laugh.

It must have been about September when I bought her out of her contract with the Uganda Government, I don't remember the time or detail but the next thing I heard was that she was in Khartoum. I subsequently found she flew up in a flying boat on one of the routine northbound flying boat services from Durban to

Kampala up to Khartoum, but of course when she got to Khartoum she was again stuck, because as previously indicated, traffic from Khartoum northbound being all priority. You had everything feeding in there; the traffic coming in from West Africa on the West Africa route and also from West Africa via the Congo, and then there was also stuff coming down from Asmara. I knew she'd got to Khartoum because the guys that used to work on the passenger counter at Airways Terminus – one of them was a local UK staff, but he had volunteered for overseas service maybe it was Johnson, or Venters – they looked after her between the two of them and saw that she had a reasonable amount of entertainment. It was several weeks that she was stuck in Khartoum, but because she was Airways wife she could stay in the Grand Hotel and it was paid for by Airways! Thank goodness for that, it saved me a lot of money!

Part of my job as the Assistant Traffic Manager was of course to keep the routes flowing as well as I could, and because of this build up of traffic in Khartoum, whenever I could get a spare aircraft to do it I was laying on extra flights to Khartoum to try and clear this backlog. I was doing fairly well and got it down to a fairly limited number, in fact probably only another day's delay. Then one morning Maxwell got very upstate because he'd found out about all these extra flights going down to Khartoum to clear backlogs in Khartoum. He thought this was terrible, wasting aircraft hours, and I said it wasn't wasting aircraft hours it was clearing priority traffic, which was one of the requirements of airlines to keep the priority traffic moving. So I put on another flight that day and what happened, sure enough, Frances was on it! But that was the last one I was able to put on, again I was very lucky indeed because after that we didn't find any more flights that were ours that we could use for these extra operations.

But at least we got Frances up to Cairo.

That is where Geoffrey's taped memoirs end. The rest of the story has been pieced together from other people's memories with a little extra information.
We don't know exactly when Frances got to Cairo: her passport 1942-47 shows an exit visa from Uganda dated 21/6/43 valid for departure before 31/7/43; a visa for Egypt issued in Uganda dated 21/6/43 valid up to 5/12/43: two Cairo Area Air Passport Control stamps with no

date but saying valid until 5/12/43; a Sudanese transit visa dated 16/7/43 issued in Khartoum with Wadi Halfa added in pencil; and an Egyptian visa extension dated 22/1/44 until 6/12/44.

So this looks as if she left Kampala in late June or July and was in Khartoum from mid-July possibly until September as Geoffrey suggests. Their first son was born the following June so she was definitely in Cairo by September. The family understood that Frances and the baby left Cairo by ship to get back to England as there was no knowledge of when Geoffrey would be sent back from Cairo.

My vague memories of the story are that there were problems leaving Cairo and that there was danger in remaining there, but Aileen Druce was able to provide more accurate information. Her husband Jimmy was Imperial Airways staff from South Africa. Jimmy was posted up to Cairo, where Aileen and Frances became good friends, especially as Frances had the new baby. Aileen explained that Jimmy had received a posting to Karachi in the autumn, but Geoffrey was suffering from ill-health, possibly dysentery or yellow fever, since he said he never had problems with malaria after his treatment in Nairobi. He was ordered back to the UK, and Jimmy Druce took over from him in Cairo, much to his and Aileen's relief, as Karachi would have been a difficult posting for them.

Frances' passport shows an Egyptian departure visa dated 5/10/44 at Port Said and arrival stamp in Liverpool dated 28/10/44. Geoffrey was, in fact, flown out of Cairo only a few days after she'd left with the baby. Frances used to say he must have flown over them in the Mediterranean, and it may have been possible, if routing via France was enabled again at that time. Geoffrey was back at his parents' home in Kent when Frances and son eventually arrived after an arduous journey via Liverpool.

Postscript

The war wasn't over, of course, when Frances, Geoffrey and baby James were safely back in England. Geoffrey returned to what was now British Overseas Airways, since Imperial Airways had been merged with other aviation interests at the start of the war. It was not long before they were demerged again, into British Overseas Airways Corporation and British European Airways. Despite his Africa experience, Geoffrey went into British European Airways, where by the early 1950s he was Cargo Sales Superintendant, supporting three young sons and a baby daughter. He had an active role in harmonisation of rules and regulations, and recalled his part in settling some difficulty over regulations in the Mediterranean area by introducing the word 'littoral' into the paperwork, so that it encompassed all those countries that bordered the Mediterranean Sea. In his archives there are the transcripts of a number of talks he gave on aspects of the new IATA regulations, including one on the Carriage of Explosives. I wonder what he would make of current restrictions.

He became Air Mail Manager in about 1963, returning to that early training in 'the mail must get through' and stowing Christmas mail bags into the first flight of *Centaurus* from Portsmouth.

In 1968, Geoffrey suffered the first in a series of heart attacks, being well treated at Harefield Hospital, where he met Alfie Pigg as he relates in his story. In fact, old airways friends littered his retirement, even after they moved to a bungalow in Dorset, where he and Frances had a happy retirement until her death in 2003, just one month short of their diamond wedding anniversary. Geoffrey coped on his own for another two years, until leaving this world to join her on 31st March 2005. Their ashes are scattered in a woodland in Hampshire, where they are pushing up bluebells together.

Appendix: Postings

Joined Imperial Airways 25 September 1933 as Commercial Trainees:
H A Durawala, Douglas Grey, John Maspero, Geoffrey Pett, Ian Scott-Hill, Ross Stainton, Sunny Sunduram, Edwin Whitfield

Movements for Geoffrey Pett
from London/Croydon Sep 1934 to Operating Croydon (Cro)
from Operating Cro Jan 1935 to Accounts Cro
from Accounts Cro 1st April 1935 to Passenger London (Lo)
from London 9 October 1935 to Brindisi by Anson G-ACRN.
   Stationed there were Denis Bustard, Pat Montague-Bates, Ross Stainton & Stephen Broad
from Brindisi 7 Aug 1936 to London 9 Aug 1936
on Leave then TMO London 31 Aug 1936
from TMO Lo 12 Sep 1936 to Rochester as Flight Clerk for takeover and delivery of F/B G-ADUT to Alexandria [*Centaurus*]
from Rochester 12 Dec 1936 to Alexandria 16 Dec 1936
from Alexandria 18 Dec 1936 to Nairobi 21 Dec 1936
[note: 2 months in Mbeya spring 1937]
S/O Pett from Nairobi 19th May 1937 to Lindi (via DAR) 26 May 1937
from Lindi 3 June 1938 to Nairobi 5 June 1938
from Nairobi 17 June 1938 to Butiaba 18 June 1938
from Butiaba 8 Sept 1938 to Juba (Rejaf) 12 Sep 1938
T/O2 Pett from Juba 22 Apr 1939 to Khartoum; Clyde Purnell was S/Supt and Pat Montague-Bates Asst S/S
from Khartoum to UK 21 June 1939 for 96 days home leave
from leave 25 Sep 1939 to Bristol
from Bristol 14 Oct 1939 to reopen Victoria Air Terminal
from UK 6 Dec 1939 to Alexandria; Stn Supt.: A Thomson till 25 May 1940, then G Pett
   Staff at Ras El Tin (Alexandria) included: T/O D Grey, T/A AJR

Murray, T/A ERF Anderson, T/A Michael Clapham. Trainees – Ken McGregor, Keith Cockerell, David Forbes, Roddy Barton, Basil Bamfylde, Oliver Hove, Bill Queckett
T/O Pett from Alexandria 16 Oct 1940 to Cairo (as Stn Supt.) from Cairo (Rod el Farag) 4 Dec 1940 to Cairo HQ; other station staff in Dec 1940 were Tr K Cockerell, T/A Gandolfo, T/O Brian Nelson
from Cairo 13 Jan 1941 to Khartoum
from Khartoum 19 Mar 1941 to Juba;
T/A O Hove was in Juba June-Aug 1941; T/O A Watts was relieving at Juba and Malakal during Sep/Oct 1941
from Juba 24 Nov 1941 to Khartoum (Wadi Saidna);
T/A Cockerell was at Khartoum Oct-Dec 1941 covering leave for various Khartoum staff. T/O B Nelson was still S/S Khartoum May 1942; Gregson, Shillitoe & Barton were also 'around' Khartoum Sept 1942; T/O G Boughton still in Khartoum Oct 1942
from Khartoum 9 Oct 1942 to Cairo; T/O D Paton at Kampala Apr 1943
from Cairo 25 Oct 1944 to UK (Lynham) posted as MCO Europe

BOAC European Region created Jan 1945 and included: Maurice Curtis (Commercial Manager) Harry Matheson (Traffic Supt. Europe) and George Boughton, Geoffrey Gibbons, Douglas Grey, Peter Shillitoe, Ian Scott-Hill and Geoffrey Pett inter alia.

Bibliography

Bluffield, Robert (2009) *Imperial Airways: The Birth of the British Airline Industry* Classic Publications/Ian Allan, London

Cassidy, Brian (2013) *Empire Flying Boat: Owners Workshop Manual – An insight into owning, servicing and flying the Short S.23 'C' Class Empire flying boat* Haynes Publishing

Cobham, Sir Alan J. (1930) *Twenty-thousand Miles in a Flying Boat: My Flight Round Africa* republished 2007 NPI Media Group

Frater, Alexander (1986) *Beyond the Blue Horizon: On the Track of Imperial Airways*. Heinemann

Knott, Richard (2011) *Flying Boats of the Empire: The Rise and Fall of the Ships of the Sky* Robert Hale, London

Ministry of Information (1946) *Merchant Airmen; The Air Ministry Account of British Civil Aviation 1939-1944* HMSO SO Code 70-481*

Munson, Kenneth (1970) *Pictorial History of BOAC and Imperial Airways*. Ian Allan, London

Ord-Hume, Arthur W J G (rep 2010) *Imperial Airways – From Early Days to BOAC* Stenlake Publishing, UK

Penrose, Harald (1980) *Wings Across the World; An Illustrated History of British Airways*. Cassell, London

Pirie, Gordon (2009) *Air Empire: British Imperial Civil Aviation, 1919-1939 (Studies in Imperialism)* Manchester University Press, UK

Sims, Phillip E. (2000) *Adventurous Empires*. Airlife Publishing, Shrewsbury, England

Index

Aba, 121
acceptance testing, 31-35
Adams, Clive, 35
aerodrome, 95.
　See also Juba aerodrome; land planes
Air Mail Manager, 208
air-conditioning, 179
aircraft:
　Atalanta (AW15), 42; Avro 9, 21; Avro Anson, 22; Avro-19, 22; Blenheim, 186; Boston, 202; Dakota, 179; De Havilland DH86, 162; HP42 - Hannibal, 36,42; HP42 - Heracles, 36,42; Leopard Moth, 56; Lockheed, 186,192; Lockheed 14, 117; Martin flying boats, 164; Satyrus, 42; Scipio class, 22, 28, 31; Solent flying boat, 156; *see also C Class flying boat*
aircraft crash, 21
aircraft trim, 32
airport resurfacing, 116
Airways Terminal, 9, 11, 20, 29, 152
Albert Nile, 98, 197
Alcock, John (Captain), 121
Aldiss lamp, 172
Alexandria, 154-160,120–1;
　Ras El Tin, 155-157
altitude test, 32
Anderson, E R F, 210

antelope, 91
Aqaba, 191
Asmara, 190
Athens, 32

baboons, 91
Bahi, Abdul, 166
Bamfylde, Basil, 210
Barclays DCNO, 58
Barton, Roddy, 210
beach landing, 55
bilharzias, 99
Blanco, John, 42
blind weather landings, 76
Bordeaux, 151
Boughton, George, 200, 210
Brackenhurst, 40
Brackley (Air Commodore), 23
Breeze, Margaret, 30
Brindisi, 22-28, 34, 128
Bristol, 148, 151
British European Airways, 248
British Overseas Airways, 181,
　See also Imperial Airways:merger
Broad, Stephen, 27, 209
buffalo, 91, 122
Burma, 151
bush country, 104
bush fire, 36
Bustard, Denis, 209
Butiaba, 55, 95, 90-93

C Class flying boat (*photos in italic*):
Calpurnia AETW, *1*, 65, *88*;
Cambria ADUV, *139*; Camilla
AEUB, i Canopus ADHL, 30, 35,
93, 94, *94*; Cavalier ADUU, 31;
Centaurus ADUT, 2, 31-35, *35*;
Centurion ADVE, *65*, 125; Circe
AETZ, *78*; Corinna AEUC, *112*,
113; Coriolanus AETV, *87*;
Corsair ADVB, 119-25, *121, 123*
Cairo, 158-62,188-92, 202-05;
 Cairo West, 108, 112; evacuation
 plans, 190; Gezira, 188;
 Heliopolis, 158, *161*, 188, 200;
 Regional HQ, 200; Rod El Farag,
 161, 188
Caledonians (Nairobi soccer team),
 40
camping, 145
Cape Town to Cairo, 97, 129, 172
carozza, 23
cataracts, 99, 103
Central Africa region, 124
centre of gravity, 30
church, 136, 187
Clapham.Michael, 210
Cockerell, Keith, 188, 210
Cole, Dick, 14
Congo, 117, 137, 163
Coussans, Paddy, 31, *94*
Crassus, Panioti, 128, 200
crocodiles, 173
Croydon Airport, 17, 31, 151;
 Rollason, 78
Crudge, Vernon, 125
Curtis, Maurice, 210

Daintree, Bill, 15
Dar Es Salaam, 56, 64
deforestation, 97
direction finding bearings, 119
discipline, 126, 142
Downing, Anthony, 14
dress code, 126
Druce, Jimmy and Aileen, 205, *206*
Durawala, H A, 12, 209
Durban, 149, 186
dysentery, 206

Earl, David, 145, *146*
East African Pilot, 64
Edwards, Peter, 42
Egglesfield (Captain), 31-35
elephant grass, 106
elephants, 91, 114;
 scratching posts, 65
Equatoria, 102, 126, 138, 172
Everitt, Elizabeth, 174

Faradge, 120, 121, 124
Faversham, 7, 144
Faversham Grammar School, 8
ferries, 199,
 See also Juba, Nile
fire engine, 7
flying boat equipment, 32
flying low, 33
Forbes, David, 210
French Equatorial Africa, 117
fresh food, 75
fuel load, 120
Fungal Mbati Wanaki, 53

Gage, "Pop", 61
Gandolfo, 210
gardenia, 197
Gezira Club, 188, *206*
Gibbons, Geoffrey, 210
gold miners, 139
golf, 39
Governor, 102, 126, 135
Governor General, 142
Gregory, Barry, 29
Gregson, 210
Grey, Douglas, 12, 190, 209, 210
guinea fowl, 128

Handover, Denis, 14, 33
Harefield Hospital, 17, 208
Haywood, Pat, 65, 70, *76*
Headquarters, Middle East forces, 25
heart problems, 17
Henderson (Airways House), 152
Hersey, Fred, 59
hippo run, 106
hippopotamus, 197
HMS Emerald, 77
Homs, 19
Horseshoe Route, 159, 191
Hotel:
    Albergo Internationale, Brindisi, 23; Avenue Hotel, Nairobi, 38; Hill Hotel, Nairobi, 38; Imperial Hotel, Kampala, 193; Juba, 101, 102, 122, 129, 130-136; Le Normandie, Le Touquet, 19; Norfolk Hotel, Nairobi, 40;

Pension Elite, Cairo, 159; Reinerheim Pension, Alexandria, 154
Hove, Oliver, 188, 200, 210
Hutchinson, Frances (Mollie), 8, 145, *146*, 153, *155*, 157-159, 184-187, 192-198, *196*, *198*, 204-206
Hutchinson, Mr, 8, 145, 159
Hutchinson, Mabel, 145, *146*

IATA, 12
IATA regulations, 208
Imperial Airways:
    Accounts Dept., 16; Airways House, 152; breakfast allowance, 20; charts, 14; Commercial Trainee, 9, 11; confidentiality, 140; evacuation, 151; Export Dept., 17; General Sales Manager, 19; General Services Manager, 12; history, 121; interviews, 9; land plane Khartoum - Juba, 171; Lisbon - Lagos,170; local employees, 49; loyalty, 13; merger, 163; permission to get married, 141; Purser, 28, 35; services, 116; South Africa route, 53; Sports & Social Club, 15; station service, 77; train connections, 22, 26; trainee pay, 11; UK - Durban, 140; UK - Kisumu, 140; unhealthy stations, 141; working hours, 128, 158
India, 151
Indian dooka, 40, 74

Ingram, John, 29
Institute of Industrial Psychology, 10
intelligence service, 24
international drivers licence, 144
Italian battleships, 24

Jinja, 98, 197
Johannesburg, 164
Juba, 36, 95, 102-118, 126-137, 163-175, 197;
  aerodrome, 128, 163-175; airport terminal, 140; catholic church, 136, 175; centre of government, 126, 130; clerical staff, 169; ferry, 100; hospital, 129; land planes, 115; Rejaf landing site, 103-117; Rejaf station, 119

Kampala, 91, 191;
  Church of Christ the King, 194
Kenya: natural history, 38
Khartoum, 176, 200, 206;
  heat, humidity, 142; Sudan Club, 141
Kikwetu, 60
Kisumu, 35
Kosti, 129
KURH, 93, 98

Lake Albert, 91, 93, 95, 130;
  fishing, 92
Lake Edward, 91
Lake Tanganyika, 91
Lake Victoria, 97, 203

Laropi, 55, 94, 130, 195, 196
Le Touquet, 18
leave (vacation), 29-31, 144-48, 191
library, 131
Lindi, 54-89, 93, 127;
  District Commissioner, 60, 80; first flying boat landing, 66; land plane, 79; native crew, 68; Officer in Charge, 59; terminal building, 70
Linstead, Bill (J), 55, 95
lions, 91
Lisbon, 151
Lloyd, Denis, 20
loading and stowage, 31
log bridge, 46
Luxor, 201

M'beriali, 79
Madagascar Channel, 186
Madge, Carlos, 31
mail:
  Christmas mail, 33; local delivery, 46; salvaged, 122; Wadi Saidna to Khartoum, 180
Malakal, 130
malaria, 91, 100, 128, 141
Manning brothers, 39
Marconi:
  communications station, 111; Radio Ops, 87; radio station, 113
maroon, 7
Marseille, 22, 33, 151
Maspero, John, 12, 209
Matheson, Harry, 210

maximum load, 120
Maxwell, Robert, 156, 160, 185, 190, 192, 202;
   wife, 198
Mbangawanga, 61
Mbeya, 42, 44-53, 194;
   catering, 47; grass cutting, 49; landing ground, 44; resthouse, 46; toilets, 47
Mbgala, 136
McCudden, Major James, 9
McGregor, Ken, 210
McHugh, Mrs, 234
meat ration, 87
Medway (river), 38
meteorology, 17
Middle East Headquarters, 111
Middlesex Hospital, 145
military officers, comparison, 130
milk float, 7
mines, 25
Mombasa, 56, 186
Mongalla, 138, 173
Montague-Bates, Pat, 209
mooring:
   buoy, 69; emergency mooring, 138, 173; laying moorings, 53, 65, 109
Moshi, 43
Mostyn (Captain), 56
Mountains of the Moon. See Rwenzori
Mt Kenya, 43
Mt Kilimanjaro, 43
Mudeeria, 130

multi-lingual, 27, 118, 164
Murchison Falls, 117, 198
Murphy, Mike, 77, 80
Murray, A J R, 210
Myercroft, Capt (SAAF), 201

NAAFI, 181
Nairobi, 38, 56
Naivasha, 55
native;
   customs - facial markings, 86; chants, 197; customs - buildings, 91; drums, 82; songs - Johnny Mbaya, 87; songs - Kwaheri, 88; villages, 83
naval drill, 81
navigation hazard, 64
Nelson, Brian, 176, 210
New York – Bermuda flights, 31
night landing, 170
night stop:
   overcrowding, 166; routine, 51
Nile, 97,
   See also Albert Nile; boat service, 156; crossing, 121; flooding, 127, 137; river banks, 128
Nile cabbage, 97
Nile perch, 92
Nimule, 95, 97, *98*, 173
normal operating height, 18

Omdurman, 145, 151, 176
Overseas Nursing Service, 185, 204
Owen Stanley Falls, 197

Pan-America Africa Ltd, 179
Parkey-Forbes, 138
Parr, Martin, 102, 170
passengers:
    handling, 27; incidents, 47, 50; necessities, 123; priority passengers, 166, 196, 199, 205; room allocation, 44
passport endorsement, 194
Paton, David, 195, 198, 210
Percival, Bob, 62, 75
Phillips (steward, Centaurus), 31
Pigg, Alfie, 18, 208
Pitts, Davidge, 20
Port Bell, 91, 118
Portuguese Man-O-War, 71
prismatic compass, 107
prison camp, 103
prison labour, 103
protocol, 135, 142;
    engraved cards, 142
psychometric tests, 10
Public Works Department, 58, 83, 85, 112
Purnell, Clyde, 209

Queckett, Bill, 210

radio:
    operator, 94, 140; tree spirits, 66
RAF, 83, 155, 161, 170, 177
Rashbrook, Len and Jean, 15
Ras El Tin, *see Alexandria*
Ray, Mark, 78

refuelling, 181
Rejaf. See Juba: Rejaf landing site;
    radio operator, 111
religion, 137
resthouse. See also Mbeya;
    Bukumi camp, 91; Government resthouse, 98, 197
Rift Valley, 37, 91
Rochester, 31, 33
Rome:
    Fiumicino, 23; Lake Vechiano, 34
Rules and Guidance for Pursers, 35
runner, hiring to send message, 193
running water, 151
Rwenzori, 194

Sabena, 117, 139, 163, 201
Sanders family: Brian, Joan, 30
Scott-Hill, Ian, 12, 209
semaphore, 155
Serengeti Plains, 41
Shell:
    barge, *81*, 96, 100, 107; refuelling, 57;
Shillitoe, Peter, 210
Shorts, 29; Stress Office, 31
SHUN, 99-100
Singapore, 185
Singh (station clerk), 44
sisal:
    decordicators, 62; estates, 62
snake bite, 46
South Africa, 151, 184

South African Air Force, 165, 172, 186;
  Transport Squadron, 177, 179, 182, 192
Southampton, 34, 151
Southern Railways Porters Club, 16, 20
special licence, 183, 193
Springer (coxswain), 99
squash, 131, 141, 188
SS Bardia, 59
SS Corynton, 91, 95
SS Lugard, 91, 96
Stainton, Ross, 12, 14, 209
Stanleyville, 50
station cars:
  Ford Model A, 144, 178; Ford V8, 39, 92, 178; Wolsey, 178
station plans, 54
station routine:
  accounting, 48; equipment, 95; operational reports, 169, 175
stivali, 128
Streatham, 11, 18
submarines, 186
Sudan, 127
Sudan Airways, 166
Sudan Government Civil Service, 102
Sudan Railways, 99, 111, 134
Sunduram, Sunny (C S), 12, 209
Swahili, 61, 76, 92, 136
swimming, 8, 15, 72, 131, 135, 142, 188

Tanga, 56
Tanganyika, 56
Tankerton, 30, 144
Teague, Bill, 159
Teheran, 192
telegraph communications, 64
telegraph station, 45
temperature. See Wadi Saidna: temperature
tennis, 73, 141
Thomson, Alistair, 160, 188, 210
Throwley, 7
Tracy, Sheila (Porch), 14, 15
trainees' reunions, 166
transporting launches and barge, 99
Travers, Dudley, 22
Trench-Thompson, Robbie, 141, 160
Tres Stilbe cigarettes, 25
tribal culture, 82-87
tuckle, or TUKL,132, *167*, 167

Uganda, 170
Uganda Railways Transport, 199

Very lights, 68, 75
Victoria, see *Airways Terminal*
Victoria station, 10, 20

Wadi Saidna, 176-180, 200; temperature, 183
Walter, Morris, 196
war:
  Battle of El Alamein, 191; boat convoy, 185; Burmese campaign,

191; civil defence forces, 147; declaration, 146; desert training, 182; phoney war, 155; reinforcements, 171; Rommel, 190; Western Desert, 164, 174, 188, 190, 201
water (filtering), 93, 99
Watts, Alan, 199, 210
weather balloon, 17
weather report, 17, 45, 111, 113, 165
White Fathers, 194
White, Stanley, 38
White, Stefani, 73
Whitfield, Edwin, 209
Whitstable, 8, 30
Wilson Airways, 38, 56
Wilson Flying Club, 38
wood fuel, 97
workman's train, 9
WRNS, 188

yellow fever, 99, 173, 206
Young, Lawrence, 160
Yugoslavian exiles, 163

zeppelin, 7

ABOUT THE AUTHOR

J M Pett studied Maths at the University of Bristol and gained a Diploma in Personnel Management while working for a major travel and transport company. After ten years as a self-employed management development consultant she retrained, gaining a Diploma in Earth Sciences from the Open University and a Masters Degree in Environmental Technology from Imperial College London. She then embarked on a policy research career, where she has many publications in topics relating to fuel poverty, energy efficiency in buildings, and climate change.

She also has a career as an author, writing as Jemima Pett. Her fantasy series for older children and teenagers, *The Princelings of the East*, comprises six titles to date, and can be found at
http://princelings.co.uk.
She also has a science fiction series for grown-ups, starting with *The Perihelix*, book 1 of the Viridian System Series,
http://viridianseries.uk.
J M Pett is an independent author, publishing works under the imprint Princelings Publications. http://www.ppbooks.co.uk

The website for this book is http://whitewaterlandings.co.uk